Sources of Control

By Anab Whitehouse

2

Table of Contents

6

Preface

The word "leadership" is, and has been for some time, a buzz word that is espoused by many to be 'the' key to solving most, if not all, of the problems in the world. If only there were the 'right' sort of leaders in the world, then the political, economic, educational, business, scientific, environmental, military, judicial, and spiritual difficulties facing humankind could be resolved.

The people in positions of power claim that they have the kind of vision in leadership with which people should be compliant, and if the latter will only cede their moral and intellectual agency to the former, then we all can have paradise on Earth. The people who are vying to acquire power maintain that the current leadership is at the heart of the world's problems and that such individuals should be replaced by those who not only understand the true nature of leadership but, as well, who have the personal qualities necessary to realize its potential.

The truth of the matter is that the desire for leadership is a pathological disorder that is engendered in others by those who already have succumbed to the malady. Leadership is a delusional belief system in which a human being believes that he or she should be given (or usurp) the authority to organize and control the lives of other human beings.

Sooner or later, the exercise of leadership inevitably will lead to war, corruption, abuse, terror, tyranny, crisis, destruction, oppression, dishonesty, secrecy, death, injustice, degradation of the environment, financial catastrophe, and the loss of humanity – both for the leaders and for those who are led. Yet, the number of political institutions, educational facilities, military programs, businesses, and religious establishments that offer courses in leadership continue to proliferate and spread their delusional propaganda.

If human beings are going to have the opportunity to solve the many problems with which we are faced, the idea of leadership needs to be eradicated from our collective consciousness. There are co-operative and consensual approaches to engaging the difficulties before us that can be effectively pursued quite independently of the issue of leadership.

Almost every day of the week, there are juries in all 50 states who – despite whatever religious, political, economic, educational, and social differences that exist among them -- are able, more often than not, to come together and solve problems co-operatively and consensually. They do this without any form of leadership ... and a jury foreperson is not a leader but a transitory facilitator whose job is not to tell the rest of the jurors how to believe or how to vote or what to do but who seeks to work with the other jurors in order to find a heuristic means through which to reach a collective judgment concerning the issues before them.

Chaos is not the opposite of leadership. The co-operation of equals stands in opposition to the idea of leadership.

However, leaders seek to convince everyone that without the presence of leadership, humankind is doomed and will list increasingly amidst the storms of life until it sinks. The argument is entirely self-serving because it is structured to place fear in the hearts of people so that the latter can be induced to cede their moral and intellectual agency to such leaders.

Dope pushers are to junkies as leaders are to followers. Leadership is about keeping the cycle of addiction going so that followers will come to believe that life is not possible or bearable without a steady supply of leadership being injected into the lives of those who have ceded their moral and intellectual agency to so-called leadership in exchange for the ecstasy of bondage.

Every human being is sovereign and has an inalienable right to seek to push back the horizons of ignorance free from interference as long as such efforts are consonant with honoring a like right in relation to others. Reconciling the boundaries of sovereignty among human beings is a dynamic, complex, and nuanced process ... a process that can only be successfully navigated by means of an exercise of co-operation among sovereign individuals and not through the leadership of the few with respect to the many.

Sovereignty is about maintaining a dynamic equilibrium. More specifically, sovereignty involves the challenge of neither seeking to control others nor permitting oneself to be controlled by them.

The following five essays explore different aspects of the pathological character of 'leadership.' Once the underlying principles of the delusional disorder are appreciated, an individual might be in a better position to realize the character of the pathology of leadership and resist its seductive, Siren-like wail.

As is the case with many of my other publications, the essays in this book can be read in any order an individual chooses. The essays are intended to be complementary to one another rather than structured in a fixed sequential, linear manner.

When Iranian students occupied the American embassy on November 4th, 1979 and, in the process, took 52 employees of the embassy hostage – and would continue to do so for the next 444 days – the actions set in motion, among other things, a wide-ranging discussion. Included among the themes of the discussion were such questions as: Why did it happen? Who was responsible? What did the leaders of the event want? Could those leaders have accomplished their purpose(s) in some other way? Were international agreements concerning the sanctity of embassy employees violated? If so, could such violations be justified? Were human rights being trampled upon? Had the United States done anything to provoke the affair? What should leaders in the United States and around the world do in response to the situation?

All of the foregoing questions, and many more, could have been asked 26 years earlier – but, for the most part were not – when Kermit Roosevelt, grandson of Teddy Roosevelt and a member of the Central Intelligence Agency, helped orchestrate a coup d'état of Iran's democratically elected government of Mohammad Mossaddeq and appointed Mohammad Reza Pahlavi, the Shah of Iran, as the new ruler of Iran and, in the process, effectively assisted him to take millions of Iranians as hostages – and would continue to do so for the next 26 years. Those who control the media get to frame world events as they please, which is why depriving Iranians of their most basic right of self-determination has been depicted by most American media as being justified in 1953 because it was said, by various leaders, that over-throwing a democratically elected government was in the interests of the United States, whereas what happened in 1979 was described by various leaders as not being in the interests of the United States and, therefore, not justified.

People's human rights were trampled upon in both cases. People were taken hostage in both cases. International law was flouted in both instances.

There were a few differences in the two cases, however. First, none of the 52 embassy employees were tortured or killed by their Iranian captors (although some of the hostages were treated roughly and kept isolated for a time), whereas thousands of Iranians were tortured and killed by the U.S. supported regime of the Shah and his infamously notorious security force: SAVAK. Secondly, the Iranians voluntarily released their hostages after a little over a year had passed, whereas the United States was not prepared to ever release the hostages it had helped the Shah to take until the United States was forced to do so by the 1979 embassy incident in Tehran.

The foregoing scenario helps to introduce several issues that will figure prominently in the remainder of the present discussion. (1) Trampling on the rights of others and taking hostages, in one form or another, is a common practice of many so-called leaders within the Muslim (and non-Muslim) community; (2) the leaders for a variety of Islamic revival movements believe – incorrectly -- that they are justified in undermining, nullifying, or controlling the God-given sovereignty of both Muslims and non-Muslims to make individual choices concerning matters of spiritual and material welfare; (3) shari'ah and Divine justice are not legal issues but give expression to matters of ontology, metaphysics, morality, identity, essential potential, and spiritual development that are best handled individually and, when necessary (i.e., when problems arise), through seeking social – not legal – consensus or mediation.

The following discussion will briefly explore some of the ideas of a number of individuals who are considered to have played an important role in pioneering various species of social reform within the Muslim world and/or with respect to Islamic revivalism. While this exploration is not meant to be definitive, it is intended to be suggestive in relation to various issues of leadership among Muslims.

Sayyid Jamal al-Din al-Afghani was a nineteenth century proponent of employing so-called 'pan-Islamic unity' as a strategy for resisting and fighting against British imperialism. While all people have a right to be free from the oppressive tentacles of imperialism – whether this imperialism is: British, American, French, German, Chinese, Japanese, Russian, Christian, Jewish, Muslim or other – the character of the tactics that are used to fulfill such an intention tend to reveal a lot about the person using those tactics as well as about the sort of "leader" that individual seeks to be.

For example, although born in Iran and educated through a Shi'a perspective, Afghani often claimed to be a Sunni from Afghanistan. The issue here is not whether he was Sunni or Shi'a – or neither – but, rather, the point is that he was willing to alter his biographical narrative as a tactical means of promoting his overall strategy concerning anti-imperialism.

In fact, there is considerable historical evidence to indicate that Afghani was not much interested in being either a Sunni or Shi'a but was, instead, committed to certain philosophical and political ideas. Religious themes were considered by him to be merely useful tools to bring about the kind of non-spiritual end in which he was interested.

Afghani sought to blaze a path that was neither rooted, on the one hand, in a blind, unthinking commitment to the sort of theological tenets and practices that populated a great deal of the traditional Muslim landscape nor, on the other hand, was he interested in a slavish subjugation to Western values, ideals and practice. Afghani believed that the 'correct' use of rationality, political/military strength, and social activism would enable Muslims – both individually and collectively – to reinterpret Islam in a manner that would effectively unite Muslims against the onslaught of British imperialism, in particular, and Western imperialism in general.

Afghani was wrong. Islam doesn't need to be re-interpreted. Islam was, during the days of Afghani, what it always has been since the time of Adam (peace be upon him), and what it is today, and what it will continue to be in the future. Islam is the Deen or spiritual way given by God to humankind so that the latter might -- with appropriate effort and if God wishes. -- find their way to, and drink from, the water of Divine Truth, wisdom and knowledge in accordance with one's primordial spiritual capacity, or fitra, to do so.

Islam is not something that needs to be reinterpreted, reformed, or revived. What needs to be refashioned are the human attitudes, practices, and ideas that serve as obstacles to the discovery of Islam's actual nature.

Discovery is a process of learning, development, spiritual maturation, and, ultimately, of Divine Grace. This process of discovery is a delicate, fragile, challenge-laden struggle.

Such discovery is not something that can be imposed on or forced on someone ... either individually or collectively. The Quranic principle that there can be no compulsion in matters of Deen is a reflection of the complex and subtle character of the process of spiritual discovery.

Afghani was also mistaken in other ways. Islam is not something to which one can reason one's way … although reason does have a role to play during the discovery process. Islam is not something that can be discovered or defended through political and military strength but, rather, Islam is eternally protected by Divinity … although individuals do have the right to resist attempts by Muslims or non-Muslims to undermine one's ability to engage the discovery process concerning the nature of Islam. Moreover, social and political activism will not, in and of itself, lead to the discovery of Islam … although social activism might be an appropriate means under the right circumstances and conditions to help protect and secure the rights of all human beings to have full sovereignty with respect to choice in relation to the process of spiritual discovery concerning the way or path or Deen that God has provided to humanity through which essential identity and capacity might be realized for purposes of learning how to worship Divinity.

In many ways, most of the foregoing points are moot as far as Afghani is concerned because he was not really interested in Islam per se. Afghani was committed to certain philosophical ideals – especially rationalism.

He believed that truth was capable of being apprehended through the scientific use of reason.

However, only an elite was capable of achieving this, while the vast majority of Muslims were limited to – and should be constrained by – a form of religious belief that maintained that misdeeds in this world would be punished in the life to come and, by conforming to such a belief system, would cause no trouble in this world for the elites who would rule over the masses.

For Afghani, the populace should be induced to unify and, thereby, provide the elite with the power and strength the latter needed to pursue philosophical truths in relative freedom. Through social activism, the masses could be shaped and directed by leaders to serve an agenda that entailed something other than the discovery of Islam or the true spiritual welfare of Muslims. Through reason, Afghani hoped to demonstrate that certain aspects of Islam could be organized to form an effective ideological buffer against the encroachment of imperialism ... a buffer that would protect the elite and create the public space necessary to enable such an elite to pursue their own ends free from the oppressive intrusion of imperialism and without being bothered by Muslims who would be preoccupied with seeking to attain salvation in the next world by not transgressing in this world.

Afghani was skeptical concerning the potential of religion. He saw it as little more than a way of helping to console people's anxiety concerning what came after death and/or as a means of comforting people with respect to the problems of this world.

However, although skeptical about the value of Islam – or, really, the value of any spiritual tradition – Afghani felt that such sentiments could be exploited if one could convince Muslims that imperialism was a threat to their way of life. Furthermore, if one enhanced the foregoing threat with the idea that imperialism was the Trojan horse through which Christianity would be forced upon Muslims, then, one might have a very effective tool for manipulating and harnessing Muslim emotions and concerns to serve other political and social ends.

Although Afghani often would paint himself in the colors of an ardent defender of Islam, he was merely camouflaging his true intentions. He considered prophets to be wielders of a craft rather than true emissaries of God. He believed that Islam was antithetical to science even though through the Qur'an's guidance concerning the importance of empirical observation and critical reflection, the Muslim world had helped transform the face of scientific practice. Moreover, he had a fairly misogynistic view of women that did not reflect the actual esteem with which women were held in the Qur'an.

As noted previously, he felt that religion had little more to offer than as a way of consoling people concerning the difficulties of life and, consequently, as something that had no solutions to the problems of life. According to Afghani, only rationalism, military strength, and social activism could provide solutions to the challenges of life.

Apparently, Afghani was intelligent, charismatic, and had some oratory skills. He used these qualities to attract some followers, but in concrete terms he was able to accomplish very little except to be able to gain access to some of the more influential social and political circles in certain localities and, thereby, have the opportunity to ply his gift of gab.

In fact, Afghani got kicked out of a number of places when, among other reasons, he ended up on the wrong side of a political crisis despite his connections. These localities included: Iran, Istanbul, Afghanistan, and Cairo.

Interestingly enough, although various pronouncements of Afghani were considered to be heretical with respect to Islam, he was never killed for espousing his views. Instead, he was escorted out of the locality.

Afghani sought to be a leader. However, his desire to be a leader was almost entirely self-serving and predicated on a need to exploit others and to control them to serve his ends.

He tried to clothe his intentions in the language of Islam, but, in point of fact he had very little understanding of Islam. To the extent that he did speak some of the language of Islam, this was used as a tactical tool to bring about Muslim unity so that he would have a power base through which to fight against British imperialism and open up the sort of free space that would enable him to pursue his own – and that of others whom he considered to be among the elite – rationalistic approach to truth.

Some people might wish to cite Afghani as a pioneer of Muslim reform and Islamic revivalism. Nevertheless, I believe that anyone who takes a closer look at his life and teachings will see that he has nothing to offer to anyone who is sincerely seeking to discover the truth about Islam.

Unfortunately, there are all too many so-called Muslim leaders who are prepared to use the language of Islam to serve agendas that are not concerned with Islam or the spiritual needs of Muslims. Indeed, Afghani belongs to the lineage of would-be leaders who are willing to exploit, oppress and rule others for the ends of the alleged "leaders", and, perhaps, that is why some people try to invoke Afghani's name as a kindred, revolutionary spirit and, in doing so, unintentionally disclose something of their own underlying, self-serving agenda with respect to Muslims and Islam.

When Afghani was in Cairo, one of the individuals who was a part of Afghani's circle was Muhammad Abduh, a student at al-Azhar University. Afghani purportedly led the circle in discussions of philosophy, law, theology, and mysticism.

Whatever Afghani's facility with philosophy, law, and theology might have been, he knew next to nothing about mysticism because he had never been a practitioner of the discipline. However, when the people who are being led are relatively ignorant about a given topic, it is amazing how wise and informed someone with the gift of gab can sound to the uninitiated.

There is evidence that Muhammad Abduh had a passing acquaintance with some aspects of the Sufi path because he had spent time in the company of an uncle, Darwish Kadr, who was reportedly a shaykh and sought to teach the young Abduh about the principles, practices, and adab of the Sufi way. Nevertheless, Abduh's time among the Sufis was fairly short-lived and, in fact, later in life Abduh came to be quite critical of this mystical tradition.

Afghani was an activist. Muhammad Abduh was influenced by Afghani to also be inclined toward political and social activism, but Abduh was more interested in reform than revolution.

At one point, Afghani's activities became too problematic, and he was expelled from Egypt. Due to Abduh's association with Afghani, the younger activist also ran into difficulties, but new opportunities arose when Abduh was appointed to be one of the editors for 'The Egyptian Gazette', an official newspaper, and later went on to become the chief editor for the publication ... a position that permitted him to wield considerable influence in framing public discussion about a variety of issues.

Eventually, Abduh's criticisms of military and political leaders, as well as his writings concerning nationalism and the British occupation led to a three year period of exile. During this hiatus, Adduh reconnected with Afghani in Paris, and the two of them formed a society and publication whose primary objective was to sound the clarion cry concerning the dangers of European imperialism and interference in the affairs of non-western peoples.

Both the society and publication came to an end. Abduh returned to Beirut where he taught young children and, as well, wrote about a variety of issues.

In time, his exile from Egypt ended, and he was appointed to one of the law courts in Egypt. Subsequently, he became part of an administrative council at al-Azhar, and, then, later on he became the Grand Mufti for Egypt. While Grand Mufti, Abduh issued a number of fatwas for individuals who came to him with a variety of problems involving legal issues and matters of morality.

Abduh was aware of the allure that European civilization had for many Muslims. For instance, Western weapons of war were superior to anything in the Muslim world, and many Muslims felt they needed to acquire Western technology in order to be able to defend their lands against further

Western encroachment. In addition, the economic wealth of the West was in stark contrast to the economic impoverishment of large parts of the Muslim world, and, again, many Muslims thought that if they imitated Western approaches to economics, that some of the 'magic' might rub off on Muslims.

War, technology, economics and politics were all fed and shaped by ideas. Some Muslims believed – quite incorrectly – that if the Muslim world would incorporate Western ideas into their lives, then perhaps, Muslims might ascend, once again, to the glory days of early Islam.

On the other hand, as much as many Muslims were dazzled and intrigued by the success of the West, it was also apparent that a considerable amount of that success was coming at the expense of Muslims whose lands and resources were being taken – through force, intrigue, or the co-opting and corruption of Muslim leaders – by Western powers. Muhammad Abduh was one of the individuals who understood that there was a basic disconnect between the lofty principles of freedom, democracy, technological progress, and economic growth espoused by the West, and the oppressive manner in which the West sought to induce the non-Western world to subsidize the materially expansive way of life that was being established in the West.

Muhammad Abduh also believed, however, that the West was not necessarily the primary reason for the problems of the Muslim world. In fact, he laid the responsibility for those problems at the feet of Muslims themselves, and he maintained that the wretched condition of Muslims was a punishment from God for having strayed from 'true' Islam.

Abduh's solution was multifaceted. He urged Muslims to be guided by the authority of the salaf or spiritual forbearers of early Islam, but he felt that all such authority should be measured against the teachings of the Qur'an.

He argued that human texts were capable of being critically questioned to determine their degree of authoritativeness. On the other hand, he believed that the Qur'an did not contain any errors and, therefore, must serve as the source of criteria for judging the spiritual authoritativeness of the texts written by human beings – even those of the salaf.

Abduh believed, however, that there could be no disagreement concerning the teachings of the Qur'an. Consequently, the Qur'an would become the means of uniting Muslims and ridding themselves of their sectarian differences, and reason would be the essential tool for ascertaining the principles and values being given expression through the Qur'an.

Through discernment of the true teachings of the Qur'an, one could become spiritually united with the understanding of the followers of Muhammad (peace be upon him). Through the use of reason and, coming to understand the actual nature of the Qur'an, all schools of theology and law, according to Abduh, would come to share a common foundation, and, as a result, the ummah or spiritual community would become united once again.

Reason is something of a will-o'-the-wisp that seems to give off a kind of light but often tends to recede as one tries to approach it and determine its true nature. Oftentimes, one person's reason is another person's insanity or nightmare, and although we all make appeals to the importance of reason, we frequently have difficulty clearly stating, or agreeing upon, just what reason is.

Furthermore, trying to use reason in conjunction with understanding the Qur'an is fraught with problems. This is not to say that reason has no place in relation to the Qur'an, but one cannot start – or end -- with reason.

In a number of places in the Qur'an, one is told that if an individual will have taqwa, or piety, then God will teach that individual. So, the starting place is a matter of taqwa, not reason.

Taqwa is more of a spiritual orientation marked by an individual's openness to, or willingness to, go in whatever direction Divinity wishes to take a person. The use of reason might have played a role in helping to shape the condition of taqwa, but taqwa cannot be reduced down to a rationalistic process since taqwa is also informed by understandings that are fed by other dimensions of human existence ... such as faith – which is not a matter of blind belief but of informed, insightful experience that comes through Divine grace – and faith (as do God's blessings) has many levels and degrees ... the faith of a Muslim is not the faith of a Momin, and neither of these is the faith of a Mohsin – that is, one who practices ihsan.

Reason is only one of the mediums through which Divine teaching takes place. Moreover, Divine logic will not necessarily be reflected in what someone considers to be an expression of impeccable reason, and, therefore, although all Divine logic is eminently rational, not all human reason resonates with such rationality.

The mind, heart, sir, kafi, and spirit – all of which are referred to in the Qur'an – do not employ the same modes of understanding, and each of these faculties are taught by Divinity in accordance with the capacity of that faculty. Reason is a function of the mind, and the mind is capable of understanding some things while it is incapable of understanding other dimensions of truth.

Unfortunately, many Muslims erroneously believe that the Qur'an can be penetrated and circumscribed by what they consider to be tools of rationality or reason. As a result, they use reason to interpret the Qur'an instead of waiting for Divinity, if God wishes, to teach them about the principles and nature of the Qur'an. Interpreting the Qur'an is a sign of impatience and lack of humility.

So, Abduh was wrong when he believed that there could be no disagreement about the Qur'an. Many people (both Muslim and non-Muslim) have a tendency to bring their own agendas to the Qur'an and filter the words of the Qur'an through that agenda, and this can lead to nothing but distortion, misunderstanding and sectarian divide. They might use the words of the Qur'an, but the Divine meanings of those words often have been corrupted, sullied, and/or distorted by human ignorance.

The Qur'an gives expression to nothing but truth. However, the interpretational methodologies and disciplines through which the Qur'an might be engaged by human beings lead to nothing but problems since the Qur'an tends to close itself – unless God wishes otherwise -- to whomever seeks to touch the Qur'an in a condition of impurity – not just physical impurity but intentional impurity and emotional impurity and mental impurity as well ... and the desire to interpret the Qur'an is but one manifestation of such impurity.

Abduh spent a considerable amount of time writing about how what he considered Islam to be was superior to Christianity. Yet, the very book that he claimed as the ultimate authority – namely, the Qur'an -- indicated that Christians were people of the Book, as were Jews ... as were the followers of other Prophets who were alluded to in the Qur'an but were not specified.

He put forth his interpretation of Christianity just as many Christians put forth their interpretations of Islam. But, in the end, all such disputes are mired in the quick-sand of arbitrary speculations and musings in which so-called rational arguments are crafted through the tools of human rather than Divine logic ... although everyone involved in the quarrel seeks to claim -- in self-serving ways and, therefore, without reliable proof -- that Divine logic is on their side of the argument.

Rather than get on with the business of life's actual purpose, Abduh, at times, allowed himself – and in the process sought to induce others to do the same – to become preoccupied with irrelevant issues of which civilization – or spiritual tradition -- was superior and which civilization – or spiritual tradition -- was inferior. The coliseums in which such battles are waged are the playground of nafs, Iblis and fools.

It doesn't matter what someone else thinks of me, or whether someone else labels me as inferior. All that matters is what God thinks of me, and this is something to which no one else is privy and that no human being can establish.

Unfortunately, when the ego is caught in the vise of pride and self-esteem, Deen, fitra, and Divine assessment tend to be forgotten. Under such circumstances, everything of real importance tends to be relegated to the sideline before the childish concerns of nafs.

In trying to argue about the purported superiority of Islam over Christianity -- or, on another front, the importance of Semitic contributions versus Aryan contributions to the greatness of a given civilization relative to another – one becomes enveloped in a war of interpretations that are entirely man-made, and, as a result, quite distant from the truth of Divinity even as the respective antagonists seek to argue that their delusional systems reflect Divine truths. Yet, Muhammad Abdu's allegedly pioneering efforts in this regard have helped frame the way in which all too many Muslims today seek to engage the spiritual problems before us.

Motivated by a massive sense of inferiority because of the material success of the West and motivated by a deep sense of self-doubt that often asks the question of themselves as much as of God: namely, how could the alleged infidel be so powerful and dominant, while the true believers (i.e., Muslims) are so oppressed and unsuccessful, the quest of many Muslims – due to the teachings of so-called leaders like Muhammad Abduh -- becomes diverted by issues of wanting to feel superior, to feel powerful, and to recapture what they perceive to be the lost glory of a by-gone age ... they want to be victorious and defeat an external foe, while ignoring the internal foe (their own nafs) that is caught up in trivialities.

What many Muslims seem to forget is that Allah has promised in the Qur'an that people's faith will be put to the test in various ways. Sometimes the test will be through wealth and riches, and sometimes the test will be through privation and constraint.

Both the West and the East have been tested through historical events. Who comes out on top in a historical sense does not necessarily reflect the spiritual calculus that God uses to assess who passed and who failed such tests.

What many Christians, Jews and Muslims often share in common is an essential ignorance about the relationship between God and human beings. That ignorance is used to "reason" about life, the world, and what should be done in relation to a series of humanitarian crises that have been brought about by delusional interpretations that reflect agendas other than Divine purpose.

Samuel Huntington was quite wrong when he talked about an irreconcilable clash of civilizations involving the West and Muslims. What makes the clash irreconcilable are the delusional systems rooted in ignorance that populate both sides and that are driving the conflict ... and Huntington, as well as people like Muhammad Abduh – each in their respective ways – has helped to perpetuate that problem of ignorance over the years.

Muhammad Abduh had been disappointed with his early encounters with education, feeling that too much emphasis was given to learning by rote and too little effort was invested in helping individuals understand the meaning and significance of what they were being required to memorize. He ran into the same kind of problem when he attended al-Azhar.

Consequently, one is somewhat perplexed when one reads about Abduh's approach to certain facets of education. For example, he maintained that the children of craftsmen and peasants should be given no more education than is necessary for them to follow in the footsteps of their parents.

According to Abduh, this meant providing such children with nothing more than summaries of Islamic teachings, along with outlines of ethical principles that indicated what was considered to be right and wrong. In addition, such children should be provided with a list of reasons as to why Islam became ascendant in the world.

Yet, we didn't come into this world primarily to become peasants or craftsmen or teachers. We came into this world to learn about and realize our relationship with Divinity, and, in effect, Abduh wanted certain classes of children to be subjected to little more than the very kind of rote learning with which he had been unhappy as a child.

Abduh believed that the curriculum for higher education should consist of, among other things, being exposed to the exegesis of the Qur'an, as well as learning about the science of Hadith, and being taught to have a rational understanding of doctrine. Again, one is confronted with the specter of rote learning in which one must simply learn and accept someone else's ideas – the accepted beliefs of the time -- about exegesis, the so-called science of hadith, and what constitutes an allegedly rational understanding of Islamic doctrine. I don't really see any focus in Abduh's approach to learning that gave emphases to assisting students to learn how to become open to being taught directly by God rather than being taught through the intermediary of human interpretations, theories, and ideas about the nature of Islam.

In the realm of politics, Abduh maintained that the ummah or community is not only the fundamental source of authority for any ruler, but, as well, the ummah is the sole determiner of what is in the best interests of the ummah, together with being the sole determiner of the means that are to be used to realize such interests. Abduh also held that rulers are not permitted to interpret the Qur'an and that rulers are to be obeyed only as long as they adhere to the requirements of the Qur'an.

Elsewhere, Abduh argued that the final authority for everything is God and His Prophet. He further stated that in Islam, there is no authority except the call to do good and condemn the evil.

The foregoing several paragraphs -- although admittedly merely a summarized overview of Abduh's perspective – seem somewhat problematic. If God and His Prophet are the final authority for everything, then it would seem that the source of a ruler's authority might be something other than the ummah. Moreover, presumably, it is God not the ummah -- Who is the

One that determines what is in the best interests of the ummah, as well as the One Who determines what is the best means through which things should be done. Is this not the whole point of revelation or guidance?

Moreover, just as a ruler is not to be obeyed if that individual deviates from the teaching of the Qur'an, so too, might one not suppose that the same principle applies to the ummah. In fact, one is a little fuzzy about just who it is, within Abduh's scheme of things, that is to establish what constitutes the true teachings of the Qur'an.

Abduh mentions that shura, or consultation, should govern the relationship between the ummah and the ruler. Yet, the precise character of this process of shura and how it is to govern the relationship between ruler and the ummah seems somewhat amorphous.

He claims that it is not necessary for people to have been trained in various disciplines of argumentation, investigatory research, or the like in order to participate in the process of shura. According to Abduh, all that is required is that people be committed to the truth and to the pursuit of what is in the public interest.

What it means to be committed to the truth is an issue of some contentiousness. Moreover, what constitutes the public interest or welfare also tends to be a very complex issue.

Does shura require unanimous consensus? Or, can shura be just a matter of simple majority? Or, is it enough that only certain elite groups be in consensus concerning such matters? And, can individuals – without prejudice -- opt out of, and not be part of, something to which others might agree? Finally, if a ruler consults with the ummah and, then, rejects or ignores the direction indicated by the shura process, has the ruler abided by the requirements of shura? Just what are the requirements of shura?

These matters are not straightforward. They have not been settled in a definitive manner – although there are some people who claim that the fundamental features of all of this were settled by the 10th century and, consequently, further deliberations were not only unnecessary but, according to such individuals, were, somehow, haram or forbidden … although I don't recall that God said any such thing in the Qur'an.

The foregoing problems are not being raised in order to argue that the idea of a Muslim community is unworkable. Rather, the problems are being raised as a way of pointing out that a great deal of additional thinking, exploration, reflection and discussion needs to take place in order to be able to have a better understanding of the possible relationships among ummah, authorities, the Qur'an, God, welfare/public interest, truth, and Shari'ah.

Abduh – and this also is true of many other Muslims – seems to want to give the impression that everything is known ahead of time ... that principles of right, wrong, truth, public interest, authority, and purpose are already known by everyone and have been agreed upon. Consequently, all we have to do is measure the conduct of a leader against the established standard and everyone will know where they stand.

The Qur'an enjoins human beings to obey the Prophet and those who have been placed in authority over one. What is less clear is whether, or not, for example what the Prophet said more than 1400 years ago should be obeyed today especially when the Prophet himself gave the order – on several occasions -- that all collections of his sayings should be destroyed. Indeed, if we are supposed to obey the Prophet Muhammad (peace be upon him) and if the Prophet indicated that one should not keep collections of Hadith, then why are we listening to Bukhari or Muslim or Dawood rather than the Prophet, and on what justifiable and convincing basis can it be argued that I am obligated to follow such sayings under such conditions?

Even if it could be undeniably established that we should consult the Hadiths, there are a great many questions about how to apply those sayings, teachings, and principles to the problems of today. When someone tells me that the Prophet, if he were physically with us today, would do things in a certain way and we can tell what that would be by consulting what he said some 1400 years ago, the question arises in me: Would I be obeying the Prophet or would I be obeying someone's interpretation of the Prophet, and if I were to obey the latter, would this necessarily be following the Prophet?

In addition, what is not clear with respect to the meaning of God's words with respect to the process of having someone placed in authority over one is just that: What does it mean to place someone in authority over another individual? The Prophets have been placed in authority over human beings. Therefore, when the former directly indicate – that is, when one is in their physical presence, or when one is given a veridical dream or spiritual encounter – that a specific individual ought to do something, then one should try to obey them.

Parents have been placed in authority over their children. But, even here, the Qur'an indicates that one is not obligated to obey one's parents if they depart from the teachings of Islam ... although there is an etiquette to such departures and, as well, there is much upon which to reflect with respect to trying to determine what it might mean to claim that one's parents had departed from the teachings of Islam.

Everyone and everything has certain rights over me. To the extent that I honor such rights,

then people and things have authority over me, and
I am obligated to obey such authority in relation to
fulfilling the structural character of the rights that
bind them and me.

My shaykh was placed in authority over me
when I became his mureed. To the best of my
ability, I sought to obey him.

Over the years, other individuals claimed to
have been placed in authority over me. However,
with time and experience I came to be skeptical
concerning such claims.

Furthermore, I am much more cautious about
whether, or not, what Divinity might have meant in
relation to the idea of placing someone in authority
over one is that this should extend to an
assortment of would-be leaders and rulers simply
because the latter individuals might have come to
power in some way. After all, power and authority
might not be co-extensive.

For example, one possible question is this: is
coming to power through whatever means
necessarily a matter of God having _actively_ placed
such people in authority, or is it merely a matter of
Allah having permitted such things to happen
without investing any Divine authority in those
individuals, and, as such, these individuals have
power but not Divinely sanctioned authority? I am
equally uncertain that what God meant in the
Qur'an with respect to obeying those who have
been placed in authority over one means that one is
required to obey whatever religious clerics, imams,

muftis, mullahs, and other such authorities say simply because they claim that they have been placed in authority over one.

Would-be leaders – both Muslim and non-Muslim -- make many claims concerning how things in society should be arranged ... about who should decide, and about how they should decide and in accordance with what criteria things should be decided and in relation to which goals decisions should be made and about what the obligations of people are with respect to such decisions. Nevertheless, it of essential importance that one not cede one's intellectual, moral and spiritual sovereignty or authority to such so-called leaders until one is completely sure – and this might never be the case -- that such a process of ceding, if it does take place, will not be betrayed, abused, or exploited ... and one only can become certain about such issues through a rigorous process of asking – and having satisfactory and complete answers be given – for an extensive variety of very pointed questions.

Besides studying jurisprudence and law in Qom, Iran, Ruhollah Khomeini also studied two other subjects, both of which were to have a tremendous influence in shaping how Khomeini understood Islam. These topics were (1) 'irfan' -- which has to do with the issue of gnosis or spiritual knowledge; and (2) 'hikmat' – which, as used and understood by Khomeini, is a form of wisdom that combines elements of, on the one hand, a system of thinking that is rooted in a form of logical scholasticism and, on the other hand, a way of seeking experiential understanding of ultimate reality.

For Khomeini, hikmat – wisdom – was the means through which irfan, or gnosis, was to be realized. By adhering to a discipline shaped by religious law as well as a set of spiritual practices, one would arrive, according to Khomeini, at a spiritual condition through which, if God wished, the individual would be 'opened' to spiritual truths.

Khomeini believed that irfan and hikmat were not antithetical to shari'ah but, in fact, were inextricably tied to Divine law. By following shari'ah one would be led to both hikmat (wisdom) and irfan (gnosis), and, as well, through kikmat and irfan one would be led to a deeper understanding of shari'ah.

There is no doubt that Khomeini was not only very knowledgeable with respect to traditional Shi'a poets, but he also knew about Sufi poets like Jalal-ud-din Rumi and Hafiz of Shiraz (may Allah be pleased with them). In fact, his familiarity with poets was such that it has been reported that a person could recite a line from almost any Sufi poet and Khomeini would be able to recite the following line. Furthermore, there is considerable evidence to indicate that Khomeini was fairly conversant with at least some of the writings of Ibn al-'Arabi (may Allah be pleased with him).

Like Ibn al-'Arabi (may Allah be pleased with him), Khomeini believed that the path to gnosis consisted of a process of purification. He broke this process down into four stages or modes of spiritual journey.

The first journey allegedly went from the human being to God. During this stage, the individual seeker of truth and ultimate reality attempts to transcend the realm of human limitations.

The second stage was said to be a journey with God through the Names and Attributes of Divinity. By means of this kind of journey, one supposedly came to understand how the Names and Attributes manifested themselves and governed different facets of reality.

The third facet of the spiritual journey involved the seeker's return to the material world and society. However, during this stage, the seeker is not separated from Divinity but is intensely aware of the Divine presence.

The fourth and final stage of the spiritual journey occurs when the seeker, after having acquired gnosis, uses that understanding and knowledge to assist others to struggle toward Divinity. According to Khomeini, one of the ways in which such assistance would be given is when the spiritually realized individual implements a government of Divine justice through which human beings will be guided toward perfection.

For Khomeini, the individual who had completed the four stages of the spiritual journey was the 'perfect' human being. Such people were the vicegerents of God and the ones who were to be placed in authority over the rest of humanity.

In essence, Khomeini's system of thought was an amalgamation of: (1) some of the teachings of ibn al-'Arabi, Rumi, Hafiz and other Sufi poets/authors (may Allah be pleased with them) concerning various aspects of transcendental mysticism; (2) Suhrawardi's philosophy of light (and this Suhrawardi is not to be confused with the Sufi mystic of the same name); (3) Avicenna's school of rationalistic philosophy, and, finally, (4) Shi'a theology. What is far less clear is whether, or not, Khomeini ever actually successfully traversed any of the four stages of the journey -- outlined previously -- to become a spiritually realized individual or perfect human being.

Many people who are intelligent can spout the theory of, say, mysticism ... and, indeed, academia is replete with these individuals. Such people can impress and dazzle many with their encyclopedic knowledge of poetry, doctrine, theory, and history, but none of this 'knowledge' necessarily means that such intellectually gifted people have realized the condition of gnosis concerning their relationship with Divinity. 'Talking the talk' of gnosis does not always entail 'walking the walk' of actually being spiritually realized.

Gnosis is not about genetically inherited intelligence. Gnosis is about the gift of experientially realized understanding that God gives to whomsoever Divinity pleases.

Furthermore, there are different modalities of human perfection. Human perfection is about the realization of primordial fitra or potential that defines one's essential nature.

There are as many different kinds of human perfection as there are created fitrahs or potentials. The perfection of the Prophets gives expression to 124,000 kinds of perfection. The perfection of the saints gives expression to countless other forms of perfection. The potential for perfection in each and every human being gives expression to still further modes of perfection.

Perfection is not about becoming God. Perfection is about fulfilling the potential that is inherent within us.

Happy is the person who is content with such perfection. Longing for any other kind of perfection will be a tawdry exercise in endless disappointment, frustration, and problems – for oneself and for others.

Consequently, even if, by the Grace of God, someone is able to realize her or his primordial potential or fitra, this does not mean such a person should assume that she or he has the right or duty to 'lead' others. To be God's vicegerent is to be a caretaker of creation, and having such duties of

42

care does not necessarily mean one should become
a political or social leader.

The individual who is a spiritually realized person has no need to seek to lead or guide others. By being who he or she essentially is, that person's mode of being a vicegerent is manifested through whatever that individual does or does not do. God uses that perfect 'tool' in whatever way Divinity pleases to serve God's purpose.

According to Khomeini, government can only be authentic when it acts in accordance with the rules of Divinity. Consequently, in order to be authentic, Khomeini believes that governments must implement shari'ah.

All too many Muslims have been brow-beaten into believing that shari'ah is purely a function of jurisprudence, legal doctrine, and legalisms. However, the Qur'an is not a legal document but a book of guidance, discernment, wisdom, example, balance, and knowledge that provides human beings with an opportunity to rigorously explore what it means to be a human being.

The Qur'an very clearly states that there can be no compulsion in matters of Deen, so just how does someone justify making government the medium through which shari'ah will be implemented and forced on the people in a given locality? The Qur'an also very clearly indicates that oppression is worse than killing, and, one wonders what could be more oppressive than when someone tries to force people to live in accordance with some given interpretation of shari'ah that reduces shari'ah down to little more than a narrowly conceived legal system.

Shari'ah is Divine Law, but this does not mean that such 'Law' must be explicated through legalistic doctrines and principles. Divine Law is the nature of the universe on all levels of Being ... material, emotional, mental, human, spiritual, and transcendental.

Shari'ah is the path that leads to a place where, if God wishes, one might be opened up to the truth – literally, to drink the waters of reality -- concerning the nature of the universe, including the nature of one's own essential self. To be sure, shari'ah is a path of purification, but there are many non-coercive, non-oppressive, and non-legalistic ways through which such purification might, God willing, be realized.

On the positive side, purification involves acquiring such qualities as: patience, courage, nobility, honesty, generosity, tolerance, integrity, friendship, forgiveness, repentance, love, steadfastness, humility, kindness, dependence (on God), longing (for God), and remembrance (of God). On the negative side, purification involves ridding oneself of such qualities as: jealousy, anger, envy, hatred, hypocrisy, deceit, selfishness, insensitivity, cruelty, resentment, arrogance, impatience, and heedlessness.

Can prayer, fasting, zakat, and hajj assist one with respect to the foregoing processes of purification? Of course, they can, but if one tries to compel people to pursue those practices, there is a very high likelihood that such compulsion and oppression will not only result in zero beneficial spiritual effects but quite possibly will have a problematic, if not destructive, spiritual impact on the people so oppressed.

Neither character nor morality can be legislated. One cannot be legally forced to develop character or to be moral since both character and morality are rooted in, among other things, having a purified niyat or intention, and methods of compulsion and oppression will never bring about such purification.

Outward behavior might be controlled through such methods, but the inner world of the heart and mind will not be so-controlled … indeed, it is human nature to be inclined to respond in problematic ways with respect to such oppressive attempts. Since spiritual progress is a matter of inward transformation not just changes in external behavior, seeking to compel people to follow a given legalistic path – even if it were correct (an assumption about which I am deeply skeptical) – is doomed to failure as a means of assisting people to realize their spiritual potential.

Does the foregoing perspective mean there should be no regulation of the public space … that there should be no attempt to protect our better selves against our lower selves? No, it doesn't, but the regulation of public space is not shari'ah.

Rather, the regulation of public space is a process of creating conditions that are conducive to people being able to choose to pursue, or not, the actual path of shari'ah without adversely affecting the right of other people to make different kinds of choices concerning how to proceed in life regarding such matters.

One of the most precious gifts – and challenges – which God gave to human beings is the right to choose. Those who wish to make shari'ah a legalistic system of coercive rules seem to believe that they have the right to take away one of the most essential gifts that God has given to human beings.

Steps do need to be taken to ensure, as best as possible, that when the personal exercise of choice spills over into the public space in a problematic or destructive way, the possible deleterious ramifications of such choices for other human beings must be constrained and limited. However, the Qur'an offers up a tremendous variety of principles for dealing with such matters that do not have to be limited to legalisms ... and, in fact, a very good argument can be made that to insist on such legalisms as the only way of regulating public space is to be oppressive with respect to the guidance and teachings of the rest of the Qur'an.

What the Prophet did with respect to the regulation of public space when he was in this world physically is one thing. But, none of us is a Prophet, and, therefore, we should not suppose that we have the wisdom, gnosis, or authority to regulate public space in the same way he did.

We have absolutely no reliable insight into, or understanding of, what went on in the mind and heart of the Prophet when he was called upon to make different decisions. We have absolutely no reliable proof that if the Prophet were physically with us today that he would decide matters in this day and age in precisely the same way as he did more than 1400 years ago.

People who seek to use only part of the Qur'an to regulate public space are not following the example of the Prophet Muhammad (peace be upon him). The Prophet's character, understanding, behavior, insight, judgment and decisions were shaped by the entire body of the Qur'an – not just a part of it -- and there are very few, if any, people living today who can claim to know how all of this would come together to shape how the Prophet might seek to resolve any given problem involving the regulation of public space if he were physically living among us in today's world.

In the '70's Khomeini sought to convince students that they had an obligation to establish an Islamic state – that is, a government that was to be ruled by Khomeini's conception of shari'ah. During this time, Khomeini also sought to persuade clerics that they had a responsibility to assume control of such a state and to ensure that the state would be regulated through the enforcement of shari'ah construed as a legal system.

47

Khomeini's justification for seeking to establish an Islamic state was rooted in the doctrine of: 'Velayat-e Faqih'. This idea has been translated in a number of different ways including: 'the guardianship of the legal jurist' and the 'theological vicegerency of the jurist'.

In turn, the notion of 'Velayat-e Faqih' is rooted in Khomeini's ideas about the four stage spiritual journey to spiritual realization that culminates in a return to society through which the spiritually realized individual, or perfect human being, sets about leading other people to perfection. All of this is very presumptuous.

Khomeini seemed to assume that he was such a perfect man. He assumed that it is the right and duty of a perfect man to tell others how to live their lives. Khomeini assumed that it is the right and duty of such a person to impose shari'ah on others and to force them to pursue a particular way of life. He further assumed that a perfect person could lead others to perfection.

I believe that the Prophet Muhammad (peace be upon him) is a perfect human being, and, yet, the Qur'an clearly indicates that the Prophet cannot guide people to the truth. Only God can lead a person to realization of the truth. Only God can open up hearts to faith and knowledge.

The Prophet is the best of examples. He is a friend and supporter and one who prays for the forgiveness of his community and for all creation. He assists people – whether Muslim or Muslim –

whenever he can and in accordance with the limitations of the sort of help that he has been permitted and enabled by God to offer. He gives counsel when asked, and, yet, he encouraged people not to ask him questions concerning Islam. Why did Khomeini believe that he could accomplish what the Prophet could not and, indeed, what was not even within the Prophet's mandate to try to do?

Ibn al-'Arabi (may Allah be pleased with him) – someone who Khomeini considered to be a perfect human being – never sought to establish an Islamic state nor did the former individual ever try to impose shari'ah (however he might have conceived it) on others. This is also true of Sufi mystics such as Rumi, Hafiz, and others (may Allah be pleased with them), and Khomeini looked favorably on all of these individuals.

However, somewhere along the line, Khomeini came to a very different conclusion than the spiritual predecessors whom he admired and quoted. This fact raises a lot of red flags concerning the legitimacy of Khomeini's understanding of many things.

Once Khomeini achieved power he proceeded to seek to purify society by ridding it of the alleged forces of evil that had been serving, in one capacity or another, as agents of the deposed Shah. The manner in which this allegedly perfect man sought to lead the evil-doers to a purified condition was not through counseling, guidance, dialogue, spiritual assistance, or the like, but, rather, he purified them by having them executed, and such executions were followed by similar purifications of other lesser officials and military personnel.

The Qur'an indicates that one is justified in killing those who spread corruption in the earth, but this doesn't mean that one must do this. Furthermore, one could engage in a rather lengthy discussion about who, exactly, was spreading corruption in the land with respect to the Iranian revolution ... especially given that the Qur'an says that if it were a matter of taking humankind to task for their transgressions against God, then not one living creature would be left on the face of the Earth (Qur'an 16: 61).

Once he ascended to power, Khomeini increasingly wanted everything under his control. He didn't do this because he was a spiritually realized individual and knew – via gnosis – what was best, but, rather, because he sought to control things and, thereby, apparently failed to realize that oppression and compulsion are not part of shari'ah.

Behavior sometimes is a good indicator of the intentions underlying it. In many ways and as the foregoing discussion suggests, Khomeini's behavior betrayed his apparent belief that he was a spiritually realized human being.

Unlike Khomeini, the example set by the Prophet Muhammad (peace be upon him) did not involve oppressively and forcibly trying to control the lives of people ... although that example did involve some instances of regulating public space in a way that resonated with the times in which, and circumstances under which, he and the rest of the community lived. Therefore, whenever a so-called leader presumes he or she has the right and authority to oppressively and forcibly control the lives of others, then one should observe due diligence in examining the theory of leadership out of which that person operates.

Hasan al-Banna, an Egyptian, was born in 1906 and passed away at the age of 43. Among other things, he founded the Muslim Brotherhood.

When he was approximately 12 years old, Banna joined a Muslim group that was concerned with issues of moral behavior. In fact, one of the primary purposes of the group was to induce its members to actively observe whatever the group considered to give expression to a strict code of Islamic behavior, and part of the inducement process was to levy fines on anyone who transgressed against that code.

A little later, he joined another group whose activities also revolved around issues of morality and bringing pressure to bear on anyone who might have erred – at least according to that group's leaders -- with respect to some aspect of moral behavior. One of the practices of this group was to send threatening letters to the alleged miscreants.

When he was thirteen, Banna became associated with a Sufi Order. This group was not only committed to following a strict code of Islamic behavior, but, as well, it had a charitable arm that sought to reform the morality of others, and Banna became actively involved with this dimension of the Sufi Order.

Although Banna developed an appreciation for certain aspects of the Sufi mystical tradition, he also had reservations about certain practices associated with some Sufi groups. On the one hand, he was attracted to what he felt was the tendency of Sufis to adhere to the moral dimension of Islam, but, on the other hand, he felt that too many innovative practices, or bid'a, had become intermingled with the Sufi path.

Without wishing to make a pronouncement one way or the other as to whether, or not, Banna was correct in his assessment of the Sufi path, a point does need to be raised with respect to the issue of bid'a or spiritual innovation. More specifically, while the Prophet Muhammad (peace be upon him) had issued warnings about the dangers of spiritual innovation, his warnings tended to be of a general nature and done without specifying that which constituted innovation.

Unfortunately, it is a common practice of all too many Muslims to try to claim that what the Prophet meant when he gave such warnings has to do with whatever the Muslims are against who are invoking the saying of the Prophet concerning spiritual innovation. If those Muslims are against music, then music becomes bi'dah, and the claim is made that this is what the Prophet had in mind when he talked about spiritual innovation. If those Muslims are against certain kinds of art, then such art becomes bi'da, and the claim is made that this is what the Prophet had in mind when he warned about spiritual innovation ... and so on.

Such Muslims might, or might not, be correct in their claims. The problem is that they don't really know what the Prophet meant when he is reported to have said what he did with respect to the issue of spiritual innovation.

The Prophet did indicate on a number of occasions that people should not make or keep collections of his sayings. So, is it an instance of spiritual innovation, or bi'da, when people seek to cite the authority of the Prophet's words to justify imposing beliefs or behavior on others?

While later in life, Banna never condemned the Sufi path, per se, he did argue that misguided Sufis should be reformed. Moreover, Banna indicated that Sufi writings should be rid of their impurities.

Determining who was a misguided Sufi and what writings needed to be cleansed were a function of Banna's judgment concerning such matters. Moreover, Banna believed that it was people such as himself who should be the ones who ought to have influential authority in relation to determining how misguided individuals and impure writings should be reformed.

Indeed, one of the facets of the Sufi path with which Banna was much enamored involved the relationship between a seeker and the shaykh or teacher. According to Banna, the connection was one of absolute obedience – a characterization with which I would take exception since I do not believe it reflects the actual nature of the relationship between a shaykh and a seeker. Banna wanted to extend this theme of absolute obedience to other kinds of relational arrangements involving so-called leaders (which he considered himself to be) and followers.

Obviously, if Banna was a leader, then the generality of people – who are defined by Banna as followers -- should obey what he, and others like him, said with respect to matters of bi'da, impure writings, and being misguided. According to Banna, it is the prerogative and right of the leader to decide, and it is the duty of follows to follow the prerogative of the leaders.

I have no problem with someone like Banna believing anything he likes. This after all is the right of sovereignty concerning the exercise of choice that God has bestowed on human beings.

I do have a problem when what someone like Banna believes spills over into the realm of behavior, and through this spill over, Banna begins to try to control me, or others, so that I, or they, become obedient to, and are compelled to serve, his vision of things. Banna presumes he has a right – nay duty -- to interfere in my life and rid me of whatever misguidance and impurities he believes me to operating through, and his justification for doing so is that he believes that he is right and that I am wrong.

Even if Banna were correct with respect to his understanding of the 'true' Islam – and this is not a foregone conclusion – there is a logical jump he is making that needs to be justified independently of being correct about something. This logical jump concerns the following question: under what circumstances, and to what extent, does someone have the right to interfere in another person's life even if one were to assume that the former person is correct and the latter person is wrong about some given issue?

The Prophet Muhammad (peace be upon him) was told through the Qur'an that it was not the Prophet's duty to guide others to the truth. Guidance belonged to Allah alone. Therefore, if the Prophet did not have the responsibility of guiding people, why does Banna believe he has the right and duty to do what the Prophet could not do?

When Banna was 21 years old, he wrote an essay to fulfill part of his educational requirements. In the essay he was critical of Sufis for withdrawing from society.

He believed that such a tendency limited their effective influence with respect to reforming society. Moreover, Banna argued that because regular teachers did not withdraw from society and, as a result, had a better opportunity to influence, change, and reform the lives of people, regular teachers were better than Sufi shaykhs. [56]

Banna's essay was predicated on the presumption that: it is the job of a teacher or Sufi shaykh to influence, change, or reform other human beings. Perhaps part of the reason why some Sufis chose to withdraw from society is because they wished to remove themselves from the temptation of trying to interfere in the lives of other people rather than focus on reforming and changing their own lives.

Banna's essay is more than a little self-serving since, at the time, he was trying to satisfy the educational requirements for becoming a teacher. Moreover, his thesis seems not to reflect his earlier experience with a Sufi Order that did promote charitable acts with respect to the needy in society.

Of course, feeding, clothing, and housing people does interfere in the lives of people. However, this kind of interference is quite a bit different than trying to change, influence, reform, or purify the way people live their lives.

The former kind of interference has always been encouraged by both the exoteric and esoteric dimensions of Islam. However, there are many cautionary considerations surrounding the latter kind of interference ... and one of these cautionary considerations is that the process of actively interfering in another person's life in order to reform or purify such individuals would seem to come in direct conflict with the Quranic teaching that there can be no compulsion in matters of Deen, and, as such, therefore, possibly qualify as an expression of bid'a.

One of the central principles in the Muslim Brotherhood that Banna established in 1928 revolved around the idea of restoring the caliphate. Banna, among others, had been appalled when earlier Kemal Ataturk had done away with the position of caliph in Turkey, and Banna believed that restoring the caliphacy would be an important means through which to reform and purify society so that it could be brought back to the true Islam.

Later on, Banna argued that politics should not be subjected to the divisiveness of a multiparty system, but, instead should be regulated through just one party. Supposedly, having just one party would be a means to unify the electorate or ummah, but Banna does not seem to have appreciated the fact that divisiveness comes from individuals not parties ... or said in another way, the divisiveness of parties is a function of the divisiveness of individuals as each, in her or his own way, seeks to find ways of controlling others to serve some agenda, and, therefore, the aforementioned divisiveness also can occur within single party systems as well as within multi-party systems.

Although Banna believed in holding elections, he believed that the people who ran for office should be restricted to certain classes of people. He felt that, on the one hand, only experts in religious law and public affairs, and, on the other hand, already established leaders of organizations, families or tribes, should be permitted to run for office.

Obviously, Banna was something of an elitist or oligarch and believed that power should be invested in a select group of individuals of whom Banna approved. Commoners, peasants, the un-empowered and women need not apply.

Indeed, Banna had a fairly repressive view of the role of women in society. He believed their activities should be restricted to motherhood, housekeeping, and staying out of sight. Consequently, he felt that women should not be taught religious law, technical sciences, or foreign languages but only those subjects that would permit them to be mothers, housekeepers, and invisible.

Apparently, among other things, Banna interpreted the Quranic ayat that men had been given a degree of superiority over women to mean that men had the right to take control of pretty much everything concerning the lives of women. However, although the Quranic ayat in question does not say in what way men had a degree of superiority over women, this has not stopped Muslim men from interpreting the passage in whatever way serves their interests, and, in the process, might be guilty of trying to introduce innovation, or bi'da into Islam.

For Banna, the government would manage all aspects of society. This control would extend from: ensuring that Islamic practices were correctly observed, to: censoring whatever books, films, songs, or ideas were considered to be antithetical to the 'true Islam'.

Banna is presuming that he and the other leaders of society know what 'true Islam' is. He also is presuming that even if he did know this that he has the right to impose such views on other human beings. What part of: 'there can be no compulsion in matters of Deen' doesn't he understand?

To be sure, society as a whole – not just government – has the challenge of determining how to proceed in a way that balances individual freedom with the need to protect the public space so that exercise of such individual freedoms do not adversely affect the capacity of others to pursue their own God-given right of sovereignty with respect to choice. This issue has a potential for being very problematic.

Nonetheless, acknowledging the existence of such a problem of social balancing does not mean that the government has the right or authority – although it might have the power to do so – to solve this problem for others and, in the process, impose its solution on the people.

Banna claims that leaders must listen to the will of the people. But, what does this really mean?

First of all, not every instance of the will of the people is necessarily in the best interests of the people, any more than one can suppose that every instance of the will of an individual is necessarily in the best interests of that person. So, how does one decide between those expressions of the will of the people that should be listened to and those expressions of the will of the people that should not be listened to?

Secondly, if it is the will of the people that should be listened to, then, why is there any need for government? Can't people carrying out their own will? If it is the will of the people that should be listened to, then why are only government leaders in charge of educating, reforming, propagandizing and purifying that will?

The way in which Banna organized the Muslim Brotherhood reveals his intentions with respect to society if he should ever gain control over the reins of government. By 1946, Banna had established a hierarchical organizational model in which Banna had control over every facet and level of the activities of the Muslim Brotherhood.

Banna ran his organization in accordance with his erroneous understanding of the relationship between a Sufi shaykh and a mureed or seeker. Namely, Banna believed that everyone in the organization owed absolute obedience to him. While he did establish a smaller and larger body of members with whom he would consult concerning matters, the final decision would be his.

The process of becoming initiated into the Brotherhood is also very revealing. Candidates were required to take an oath of commitment to Banna's conception of jihad in which a person should be willing to seek out death and martyrdom as he sought to convert the world to Banna's ideological stance concerning Islam.

The foregoing oath of commitment was taken in a darkened room. During the ceremony, the would-be initiate had to swear secrecy concerning the Brotherhood while his hand was on a Qur'an and a pistol.

The pistol is a multi-faceted symbol. On the one hand, it implies a willingness to use force to carry out the agenda of the Brotherhood, and, on the other hand, it implies what lays in store for anyone who violates the oath of secrecy or the demand for absolute obedience.

Considered from another perspective, the use of both a pistol and the Qur'an in the initiation ceremony suggests a deep-rooted lack of faith in God. Among other things, the presence of the pistol tends to indicate that Banna seemed to believe that the Qur'an, by itself, was not considered a sufficiently adequate focus of loyalty, commitment or solution to life's problems.

According to Banna, the purpose of the Brotherhood was to offer assistance to the rulers. The form of this assistance concerned advising the ruler how to run the country in accordance with the ideals of 'true Islam'.

Nevertheless, Banna also indicated that the Brotherhood should be prepared to use force if the rulers proved to be intransigent with respect to the 'advice' or 'counsel' that was being offered through the Brotherhood. In other words, his position seemed to be: 'listen or else', and as someone once told me, if you can't hear no, then, what one is asking is not a request or a mere giving of advice and counsel.

The fact of the matter is that at times violence was employed by the Brotherhood, not only with respect to the government but, as well, in relation to individuals with whom the Brotherhood considered to be purveyors of something other than the 'true Islam'. This willingness to resort to violence if one doesn't get what one wants is a very slippery slope that very quickly ends up justifying all manner of acts of cruelty, brutality, and oppression.

Banna wanted to return to the teachings of the salaf, the spiritual forbearers of early Islam. However, his motives for wishing to do so are somewhat muddled.

On the one hand, he blamed the condition of the Muslim world -- vis-à-vis being in a position of degrading subjugation to Western imperialism and colonialism -- on the fact that Muslims had strayed from the teachings of 'true Islam'. Banna argued that the salaf adhered completely to 'true Islam' and, as a result they were rewarded with control of a large part of the known world at that time.

Banna believed that if Muslims were brought back to the 'true Islam', then Muslims would, once again be rewarded by God – as he believed had been the case in relation to the salaf -- with control of the world and, in the process, would be permitted to throw off the shackles of Western oppression. Unfortunately, by thinking in this manner, Banna has muddied the waters of intention in which what is done by a Muslim should be done for the sake of Allah and not for the sake of any advantageous rewards or ramifications that might come from this.

The Muslim Brotherhood might have accomplished any number of good things such as: assisting the needy, feeding the poor, building schools, physically cleaning up neighborhoods, and helping the sick. However, such good deeds always had a hidden price and cost in which sooner, or later, people would be expected to pay for those good deeds by ceding their moral, intellectual, and spiritual authority to the leaders of the Brotherhood.

If God wishes, true Islam teaches individuals how not to cede their moral, intellectual, and spiritual authority to anyone but God. If God wishes, true Islam teaches individuals that one does not need to commit oneself to the way of God with one's hand on a pistol and that the Qur'an, alone, is more than adequate. If God wishes, true Islam teaches individuals that while we have duties of care to others, nevertheless, seeking to fulfill such duties does not entitle one to absolute obedience from others. If God wishes, true Islam teaches individuals that trying to convert others to Islam is not one of the pillars of Islam and that the inclination of hearts to Islam is the business of God, not of human beings. If God wishes, true Islam teaches individuals that one should have some degree of humility with respect to the correctness of one's understanding of the truth and that just because one believes one is right, this does not justify one's trying to impose one's beliefs on others. If God wishes, true Islam teaches individuals that there can be no compulsion in matters of Deen, and, therefore, to whatever extent one uses compulsion, force, and oppression in order to induce someone to adhere to one's interpretation of the 'true Islam', then, one is violating one of the basic tenets of Islam.

Given the foregoing, I am of the opinion that there is a great deal about the 'true Islam' with which Banna was not familiar. Given the foregoing, I am inclined, God willing, to be prepared never to cede my intellectual, moral, and spiritual authority to would-be leaders like Banna who tend to filter reality through their own high opinion of themselves and believe they have been given Divine sanction to proceed in a direction that, unfortunately, seems far more likely to take people away from the 'true Islam' than toward it.

<u>*A Western Approach to Leadership*</u>

[The following essay is a critical response to: "New Insights about Leadership," an article that can be found in the *Scientific American*'s magazine: <u>*Mind*</u>. That piece is authored by: Stephen D. Reicher, S. Alexander Haslam and Michael J. Platow.]

Traditional theories of leadership center on issues such as charisma, intelligence, and other personality traits. According to such theories, 'leaders' utilize the inborn qualities that are believed to be at the heart of leadership – whatever one's theory of leadership might be -- in order to apply that quality of 'leadership' to an audience in order to induce the members of target-audience to pursue whatever behavior, ideas, or policies are desired by the leader .

The induction process occurs when a 'leader' instills the individual members of the target audience with a sense of: will power, dedication, motivation, and/or emotional orientation that the members of a given set of people would not have – according to the leader -- in the absence of such assistance. The justification for pursuing such an induction process is to: (a) help a given set of people to accomplish more than it would have without assistance from a leader; and/or (b) to

assist a given set of people to realize what is
believed to be in the best interests of those people.

Whether, or not, that which is to be
accomplished by such a set of people is good thing
is another matter. Similarly, whether, or not, that
which is to be realized through the assistance of
such a leader is truly in the best interests of the
people being 'assisted' in such circumstances gives
rise to another set of issues and questions other
than that of the idea of leadership considered in
and of itself.

New theories of leadership postulate that the
'leader' is someone who works to come to
understand the beliefs, ideas, values, and interests
of the followers in order to lay the groundwork for
an effective dialogue through which one will be
able to identify how the group should act.

The foregoing idea reminds me of the
Communist dictum – 'From each according to his
ability, to each according to his need.' I once asked
a person who spouted the foregoing maxim about
the problem of who would be the one to determine
'ability' or 'need', and in accordance with what
criteria would such determinations be made ... and
we might just note in passing that the maxim is not
gender neutral. The individual to whom my query
was directed was unable to answer my question
although he was reported to be quite
knowledgeable about communism.

Just as questions can be asked about the
identity of the members of a classless society who

are supposed to give us 'objective' answers to the nature of 'ability' and 'need', so too, one might raise questions about the character of the dialogical means through which one will arrive at solutions to the question of what are to be the ways in which a given group should act. For example, who will be the one to determine what the beliefs, values, and interests of the 'followers' are or should be? What methods will be used? What theories will shape such considerations? How does one know that what the masses believe and value ought to be what is pursued en masse? How does one establish a dialogue between the one and the many, especially when the many are not likely to all believe the same things or value the same things? If the masses already have beliefs and values, then what need is there for leaders to identify those ideas and values in order to get people to act in certain ways? Aren't the people already acting on such beliefs and values independently of 'leaders', and if they are not, then doesn't this suggest that the beliefs and values that might actually be governing behavior are other than what was being professed? And, if so, in which direction should the leaders seek to influence the followers, and what justifies any of this?

The idea of having a real dialog between the one (the leader) and the many strikes me as odd. If a leader has the power or ability to determine which parts of the dialog will be enacted or dismissed, then I am not really sure that we are talking about the notion of dialog in, say, Martin

Buber's sense of an 'I-thou' relationship in which the two facets of the dialog both enjoy an equal set of rights (with concomitant duties to respect the rights of the other) and are co-participants in the sacredness of life -- however one wishes to characterize such sacredness (that is, in spiritual terms or in humanistic terms).

It is possible to have leaderless groups who engage in a multi-log in order to reach a consensus about how to proceed in any given matter. Within this sort of leaderless group, there might be "elders" who have earned the respect of the other members of the group because of the insight, skills, intelligence, talents, and/or abilities of those "elders', but the function of these elders is not to direct a discussion toward some predetermined goal, purpose, or outcome, but, rather, their function is the same as everyone else's function within the set of people engaging one another – namely, to enrich the discussion and, thereby, try to ensure that all aspects of a question, problem, or issue have been explored with due diligence.

Many indigenous peoples often operated through such leaderless groups. Westernized people – who tend to insist that any collective or group of people must have a leader or head person – frequently mischaracterized the elders of some indigenous peoples as being leaders in a Western sense and, therefore, as individuals who had characteristics and functions comparable to the leaders in non-indigenous groups or societies when this was not always so.

In such leaderless groups, the set of people as a whole decide actions through consensus. In other words, through an extended multi-log (which might take place in one setting or over a period of time) every member of the group either comes to see the wisdom of collectively moving in a certain way – a way to which all of the members of the group have contributed in and helped shape -- or the group as a whole does not reach a consensus and everyone has the right, without prejudice, to refrain from participating in any collective action that some lesser portion of the whole might take.

A central principle in some modern theories of leadership is, supposedly, to have leaders try to influence followers to do what the latter individuals really want to do rather than trying to impose things on the followers through the application of various forms of carrot-and-stick stratagems. However, one might raise the following question concerning such an alleged central principle: If someone really wants to do something, then why aren't they doing it? What is holding them back? Is that which is restraining them something that is constructive or destructive? Is that which the 'followers' allegedly really want to do something that is constructive or destructive? What are the criteria, methods, and processes of evaluation that are to be used in sorting this all out?

According to some the new theories of leadership, a leader needs to position himself or herself among the people to get the latter to believe that the leader is one of them. If, or when, a "leader" is able to become positioned in such a manner, the belief in such theories is that this will help the leader to gain credibility among the people. That credibility can be used to leverage group behavior.

However, it is an oxymoron to say that a leader is one of the people. After all, there is a reason why two different terms are being used to refer to the two sides of the equation.

The leader is not one of the people, but, rather, is just someone who is trying to induce people to believe that she or he is one of them. If the leader were truly one of the people, then that person would not be in a position to determine what course of action is to be pursued by the set of people being led.

Situations in which sincere multi-logs occur do not have leaders or followers. There are only participants, all of whom are equal with respect to rights and duties concerning such rights\ -- although there might be one, or more, elders within the set of people engaging one another whose ideas might be valued without making the following of such ideas obligatory or mandatory with respect to other participants. The contributions of such elders are valued without necessarily being determinate in relation to the outcome of any given discussion.

Let's return to the perspective of some of the newer theories of leadership in which one of the tasks of a would-be leader is become positioned so as to be viewed as one of the people so that credibility can be established in order to leverage the group in one direction rather than another. How does one know that the values and beliefs of a leader are really the same as those of the followers? What are the criteria, methods, and process of evaluation that are to be used in determining that the ideas and values of a leader and the 'followers' are coextensive?

Isn't it possible that a leader might profess to being committed to certain kinds of beliefs and values in order to garner the support from the people that will generate an apparent mandate to permit the so-called leader to do whatever he or she wishes and, then attempt to argue that whatever such leaders do is an expression of what the people really want? More importantly, how could any given leader credibly claim that she or he shares the same beliefs and values as the followers when every group tends to be highly disparate in many ways when it comes to such beliefs and values?

Not all Blacks think in the same manner, or feel about issues in the same way, or share the same values. This feature of diversity also is true of Catholics, Protestants, Jews, Muslims, Democrats, Republicans, Socialists or any other group or collective one cares to mention.

At any given instance, a leader's values and beliefs might coincide with some of the beliefs and values of the 'followers", but the two sides will never be coextensive. This is why politicians often tend to speak to various groups in different ways in order to induce the latter individuals to believe that the 'leader' is one of them, and, then when the election is won, the leader can't possibly act in ways or advocate values with which everyone who 'followed' that person (by voting for them) might agree.

From the perspective of the most recent theories of leadership, being a leader is not a matter of possessing certain kinds of personality characteristics. Instead, being a leader is a matter of learning the art of how to be a chameleon and, thereby, seem to blend in with any given crowd. The fact of the matter is that a leader could even appear to act in ways that reflect the likes of the followers without any need to actually be the sort of individual that is being projected to the crowd.

Naturally, when, as a result of keeping track of the actual behavior of leaders, people begin to see that there is a distinct difference between, on the one hand, what they -- the general membership -- tend to believe or value and, on the other hand, what the leaders believe and value, then conflicts and tensions tend to proliferate. This is where press secretaries and the other spin-masters enter stage right in order to smooth over such differences and, perhaps, to even re-frame such

differences as supposedly being what the people
actually needed and wanted.

Drawing a distinction between a collective and
a group, at this point, might be of some assistance.
A collective is an aggregate of people that is
operating within a diffuse or defined framework,
and this aggregate of people might not all be
operating within such a framework willingly or
they might be 'participating' in ways that generate
friction, tension, or conflict within the collective as
a reflection of such a dimension of unwillingness.

A group, on the other hand, is a segment of a
collective that has come together willingly to serve
or achieve a particular purpose or set of purposes.
Oftentimes, although not necessarily, groups
operate through consensus – that is, requiring
unanimous agreement for action to take place –
and when consensus is present, the group is a said
to be coherent or unified in its purposes.

Because of the logistical problems surrounding
the process of reaching a consensus, most groups
tend to be small. However, the meaning of 'small'
might vary with the character of conditions
prevailing at a given point in time.

Groups, unlike collectives, often tend to be
sensitive to temporal conditions. In other words,
groups tend to come together for only a limited
time and for limited purposes. When the time
and/or the purpose(s) characterizing such a group
expire, then, oftentimes, the group might expire as
well. As such, groups tend to arise out of, and

dissolve back into, a backdrop of collective dynamics involving various historical, social, economic, spiritual, ecological, psychological, philosophical, technical, scientific, legal, and political forces.

To the extent that a set of people is not unified, then that group is not coherent. Incoherent groups tend to be given to friction, conflict, tension, altercation, fragmentation, and dissolution.

Whether a set of people is considered to be a collective or an incoherent group might depend, in part, on the degree to which people are willing or unwilling participants in what is transpiring. Moreover, whether a set of people is considered to be a collective or an incoherent group might also depend on the extent to which such individuals have been induced to cede their moral and intellectual authority to other individuals within the set of people being considered (and there will be more on this issue of ceding moral and intellectual authority shortly).

Coherent groups usually do not need leaders ... although there might be elders within the group whose ideas, values, and talents might be respected and utilized without making such a person a leader. Providing constructive contributions to a group that helps enable a set of people to achieve their goals and purposes is not the same thing as being a leader.

Different circumstances, projects, problems, and so on might come to feature the expertise, wisdom, or abilities of different people within a social setting. It is the quality of contributions that are recognized by other members of the group that come to identify someone as an 'elder', and as various people within a set of people contribute across time, the identity of the elders who play influential roles in any given set of circumstances might change.

Some elders might have the capacity to identify talent and abilities in other people within a group. By advancing the names of other people so that the potential of these individuals can be drawn out to serve the purposes and goals of a group, the 'human resource elder' is not being a leader but is, instead, simply making constructive contributions in accordance with her or his abilities in order to help further a group's purposes.

The wisdom exhibited by any given group often is a direct function of the diversity inherent in that group. However, diversity, in and of itself, is not enough to generate wisdom with respect to any action that a group might take, and, therefore, one also must take into consideration the quality of the diversity that is present in any given set of circumstances.

Not all collectives constitute groups ... even incoherent ones. A nation tends to be a collective that consists of a variety of coherent and incoherent groups, as well as any number of non-aligned individuals. A government tends to be a collective that consists of a variety of coherent and incoherent groups, along with any number of non-aligned individuals. A schooling system tends to consist of a variety of coherent and incoherent groups, together with any number of non-aligned individuals. An economy is a collective that consists of an array of coherent and incoherent groups, as well as any number of non-aligned individuals. Many corporations – especially publically traded entities – tend to consist of a variety of coherent and incoherent corporations, along with any number of non-aligned individuals, and, in addition, the bigger a company is, the more likely it is to be a collective rather than a group.

In addition, one should draw a distinction between, on the one hand, a goal or purpose, and, on the other hand, an agenda. A goal or purpose is self-contained and does not extend beyond the essential character of the goal or purpose being pursued, whereas, an agenda is a process that seeks to usurp the goals and purposes of another to serve some end that is independent of such a goal or purpose.

For example, seeking to feed the hungry is a goal or purpose. Using the former activity – that is, feeding the hungry -- to help bring a person to power constitutes an agenda.

Specific goals and purposes are what they are. They are not intended to extend beyond the character of a given purpose or goal – although, on occasion, the pursuing of one goal or purpose might have ramifications for other aspects of a social setting that were not originally intended when such a goal or purpose was originally envisioned.

Agendas, on the other hand, usually extend beyond the context of some given purpose or goal. Furthermore, agendas tend to involve techniques and strategies of undue influence that are intended to illicitly persuade – and, thereby, exploit -- someone with respect to the issue of ceding away an individual's moral and intellectual authority to another human being. As such, agendas are used to re-frame social settings to induce people into believing that they are striving for one thing when, in reality, those people are being manipulated into serving some other purpose or set of purposes. The more narrowly defined purpose is the 'Trojan Horse' through which a hidden agenda gains access to people's original intentions and destroys those people in the process.

The intellectual aspect of one's essential, existential authority gives expression to one's capacity to search for, and within certain limits, either find truth or to peel away that which is not true and, thereby, establish a closer, if rather complex, relationship with the nature of truth in a given set of circumstances. The moral facet of one's essential, existential authority entails an individual's sincere struggle to act in accordance with one's understanding of the nature of truth at any given point in time.

The way in which a person attempts to do due diligence with respect to her or his moral and intellectual authority might not always be correct. Mistakes might be made and errors committed with respect to the exercise of either moral and/or intellectual authority.

However, if such mistakes and errors are the result of sincere efforts, an individual will continue to struggle to shape the exercise of moral and intellectual authority into a process of learning through which that person has the opportunity to develop a rich, experience-based wisdom. Ceding one's moral and intellectual authority to another short-circuits the learning process and prevents one from developing wisdom in relation to improving one exercise of one's moral and intellectual authority as one engages, and is engaged, by life's experiences.

Techniques and strategies of undue influence are designed to obstruct, undermine, or co-opt an individual's efforts to struggle toward realizing either one's intellectual authority and/or one's moral authority. In addition, techniques and strategies of undue influence seek to induce people to be willing to cede their moral and intellectual authority to another individual, group, organization, party, or government thereby enabling the latter 'entity' to draw upon the ceded authority to 'legitimize' or 'rationalize' some given action, policy or agenda.

The more people there are who can be induced to cede their moral and intellectual authority to such an individual, group, organization, party or government, then the more powerful does the latter become. In fact, such power becomes one more tool in the arsenal of undue influence to broaden its sphere of control over other individuals who might not have ceded their moral and intellectual authority but whose ability to resist the exercise of that power which is rooted in ceded authority because the former is often severely attenuated and out-flanked.

Acquiring power through collecting the ceded moral and intellectual authority of others can never be justified even when constructive results might ensue through the use of such ceded authority. Such acquired power can never be justified because it is predicated on usurping the most essential dimension of what it means to be a human being, and sooner or later, the continued use of the power acquired through ceded authority will destroy not only individuals but the social setting as well, and history bears witness to this existential principle.

Working for a specific goal or purpose does not generally require anyone to cede his or her moral and intellectual authority to other human beings because the individual tends to be actively and directly involved with the goal or purpose being considered in a way in which that individual has full control over his or her moral and intellectual authority as they act. In other words, the goal or purpose gives expression to a person's moral and intellectual understanding of the way things should be, and, therefore, serves the given purpose or strives toward realizing a given goal in concert with that individual's direct exercise of his or her moral and intellectual authority.

One does not have to cede one's moral and intellectual authority in order to be able to work in co-operation with other people who also are operating in accordance with their own commitment to observing due diligence in relation to exercising their moral and intellectual authority as responsible agents in the world. Reciprocity is one of the key features of people who are in harmony with one another as they maintain control over their respective spheres of moral and intellectual authority while acting as independent agents in a social setting. The reciprocity is a reflection of the way in which the independent agents within the group or social setting tend to honor the right and responsibility of other people to exercise due diligence with respect to their respective capacities to serve as sources for moral and intellectual authority.

Agendas, on the other hand, are almost entirely devoid of considerations of reciprocity except in ways that have been reframed to make the relationship between a leader and the followers seem more equitable or appear more given to reciprocity than actually is the case. Those who push agendas rarely, if ever, are interested in working with people in order to ensure that the moral and intellectual authority of the latter is protected, preserved, and/or enhanced because doing this would tend to be counterproductive to and individual, organization, party, or government being able to push through an agenda.

To be able to successfully pursue an agenda, one needs: either raw power – in the form of brute force -- or one needs the power that is acquired through inducing people to cede their moral and intellectual authority. The latter form of power seems more civilized than the exercise of brute force – whether in the form of an individual enforcer, or in the form of militaristic, legal, or governmental enforcement – but using the power acquired through inducing people to cede their moral and intellectual authority is, in the long run, every bit as destructive and unjustifiable as is the exercise of brute force to realize some given agenda.

When a person is not willing to cede his or her moral and intellectual authority, then such an individual recognizes and understands that the authority for any action issues from, or is rooted in, the person and does not issue from, nor is it rooted in, anyone else. When a person cedes her or his moral and intellectual authority, then such an individual is vesting that authority in another human being, group, institution, organization, party, or government to enable the latter to make decisions on behalf of the person who is ceding that authority. Furthermore, the individual who is ceding moral and intellectual authority to another human being tends to feel and to believe that she or he is no longer required to be a guardian over, or exercise due diligence with respect to, how such authority is actually being used.

Having moral and intellectual authority is a birthright. This is true from a spiritual, as well as a humanistic, perspective.

To have such authority means that one is responsible for exercising due diligence both intellectually and morally to ensure, to the best of one's capabilities, that what one is doing does not harm, undermine, or compromise anyone else's capacity for exercising similar authority in relation to her or his own life. To cede such authority to others means that one has been induced to abdicate the throne, so to speak, of one's own individual kingdom -- together with the authority that is, by birthright, vested in such a kingdom – and, thereby, to turn over that authority to another human being to dispose of as the latter individual judges to be appropriate.

When ceded moral and intellectual authority leads to empowerment of some other individual, organization, party, or government, such empowerment will inevitably be turned back upon the source from which that power originally was derived (i.e., the one who has been induced to cede moral and intellectual authority) in order to try to convince that source that she or he never had a right to such authority to begin with. Techniques of undue influence (involving the media, schooling, government policy, theories of jurisprudence, religious institutions, and various forms of social pressure) will be employed to keep individuals disengaged from their inherent right to observe due diligence with respect to the exercise of moral and intellectual authority.

Since the time of Max Weber, many people have been captivated by the idea of "charismatic leadership". A charismatic leader is someone who, supposedly, is to serve as a savior of some kind ... an individual who will solve the maladies of a tribe, group, or collective ... the one who will lead humanity to some mythical utopia.

When, historically speaking, so many 'charismatic leaders' turned out to be oppressive, self-aggrandizing, murdering, self-serving tyrants, then some people began to sour on the underlying traditional idea of leadership that was rooted in the notion that leadership is a function of personality traits of one kind or another that are inherent in the leader. Some of those who were dissatisfied with traditional approaches to the notion of leadership, went in search of some other, hopefully more fertile ground in which to plant the seed of leadership

For example, some people came up with the idea that the best leaders are those who give the impression that they are part of a set of people and, as leaders, are only really interested in helping people to get what they want and, as leaders, to act in ways that will allow people to realize that which the people actually desire. This is referred to as a "contingency model" because the concept of leadership is considered to be a function of the context in which a so-called leader operates.

Traditional models of leadership claimed that leaders were individuals who could overcome problematic circumstances through the manner in which they imposed their will on, or did their charismatic magic in relation to, such problems. Newer models of leadership maintain that it is the nature of the circumstances that will determine who will be a successful leader.

'Contingency model-approaches' to leadership maintain that every context involves one, or more, challenge for the exercise of appropriate leadership. Being able to successfully navigate such challenges suggests that there might be an optimum match between the nature of a contextually-based challenge and the qualities that a leader should exhibit in order for the latter for an individual to meet the challenge of leadership that is posed by a given set of circumstances. In other words, according to some of the newer theories of leadership, only a person with a certain kind of skill set will be able to succeed in any given set of circumstances involving a challenge of leadership.

To claim that every set of social or group circumstances poses challenges of leadership, is to frame discussion in a particular way. In other words, if one assumes that whatever problems arise in a group or social setting give expression to one, or more, challenges of leadership, then this is to automatically assume that all problems must be filtered through the idea of leadership in order to deal with those problems.

If, on the other hand, one were to argue that whatever problems arise within a social or group setting poses a challenge for the members of that setting, and in the process, one excluded any considerations of leadership from being part of possible proposed solutions, then one might begin to think about how to try to resolve such problems in ways that do not recognize the concept of a 'leader' in any traditional sense that requires one to make a distinction between leaders and followers with concomitant differences in assigned roles.

In the newer theories of leadership much depends on how one characterizes the nature of the leadership challenge that exists in a given set of circumstances. In addition, much will depend on how one believes those challenges might be best met ... or, even what one believes the criteria are for determining what constitutes 'best meeting' such challenges ... or, what one believes about whose perspective should be defining the criteria and methods for determining what might be meant by the idea of ' being best met'.

To say that circumstances or context provide the criteria for understanding the nature of leadership is to ignore the question of who gets to 'frame' those circumstances in terms of what the latter supposedly are about, involve, or mean. More importantly, and as outlined earlier, the new approach to leadership is predicated on the unquestioned premise that leaders are either necessary or even desirable in any given situation.

The authors of the *Scientific American Mind* article on 'leadership' believe that there is a symbiotic relationship between a leader and the followers who make up a set of social circumstances. This presumes that the dynamic involving: leaders and followers, is necessarily symbiotic rather than, for example, possibly parasitic in character, and this is a questionable presumption.

Newer theories of leadership give emphasis to the importance of having insight into the dynamics of group psychology. In other words, every individual participates in groups from which facets of identity are derived – namely, social identity. This aspect of identity is part of what makes group behavior possible since as different individuals identify with a given group and such a group acts in certain ways, individual behavior will be shaped by what goes on in the group.

However, what if someone raises the question of whether identifying with a group or permitting a person's behavior to be shaped by a group are necessarily good things? What if the self-realization of a person -- and, quite irrespective of whether one construes the idea of self-realization in spiritual or humanistic terms – depends on establishing an individual's sense of self quite independently of groups? What if the requirements of morality require an individual to swim against the currents inherent in the flow of group dynamics?

To be sure, human beings have a social dimension to them. We need other human beings to develop physically or emotionally in a healthy way, and we need other human beings to be able to, for example, learn to speak a language, and we need other human beings to be able to learn how to navigate through, and survive in, waters that are populated by the presence of other people. Furthermore, there is no doubt that many, if not most people, tend to filter their sense of self through the lenses provided by various groups.

Nonetheless, none of the foregoing admissions require one to say that one's sense of identity should be a function of groups. Furthermore, none of the foregoing admissions requires one to contend that group dynamics is always a constructive force, nor do any of the foregoing admissions demonstrate that one does not have an obligation to oneself -- and, perhaps, even to the truth of things -- to resist the tendency of groups to want to impose themselves on individuals in oppressive, destructive ways.

To claim that group behavior is only possible when everyone in the group shares the same goals, interests, values, and understandings is a contentious claim. In many societies and groups there are an array of negotiated, mediated, adjudicated, and electoral modes of settlement that are accepted not because everyone shares the same interests, values and understandings, but because the participants have some degree of, at least, minimal commitment to a framework of rules and procedures through which agreements will be reached that while not entirely satisfactory, nevertheless, such agreements do have enough points of attractiveness that will enable the collective to proceed to interact in somewhat cooperative ways, despite whatever dimensions of friction and disharmony might be present.

How different people understand the underlying framework of principles, rules, and procedures that are being alluded to above and that govern such processes might be quite varied. Disputes and conflicts might arise because of these sorts of hermeneutical differences, and, as a result, problems tend to proliferate. At that point, groups might come together and try to utilize the underlying procedural framework, once again, as a way to try to sort things out ... not because everyone agrees on the meaning, value, or purpose of that framework but because they don't have an alternative to such a system ... unless , of course, a given community, society, or nation reaches a tipping point in which the participants believe that revolution – whether peaceful or violent – is the only way of trying to find a more equitable, logical, practical, and effective way of doing social things.

Leaders tend to be the gate-keepers of the different modalities for: mediating, negotiating, or adjudicating settlements within a given framework of group-dynamics. The power and authority of these leaders tends to be derived, in some sense, from such a system, and, therefore, leaders have a vested interest in maintaining that kind of system quite independently of whether, or not, that system actually serves the needs of the people whose behavior and ideas are being shaped, framed, and filtered by that system.

The reason why leaders often need to resort to an understanding of group psychology is so they can determine the fulcrum points in society that when leveraged will be capable of moving the members of a groups in directions that either will maintain the status quo or will advance the agenda of the leadership. If a leader can convince the 'followers' that he or she is one of them, and if the leader can identify the appropriate tipping points within such a group of followers, then the credibility that is derived from identifying oneself with the group's sense of self will permit a leader to leverage such credibility to move the group in a desired direction – not because this is what they group necessarily really needs but because the group is 'led' to believe that such a direction is what the group has wanted all along or is in the 'best interests' of the group.

Part of the process of the new approach to leadership involves techniques of persuasion that are designed to induce people to identify with particular groups and to induce such individuals to believe that the Interests, values, and beliefs of the group are their own interests, values and beliefs. These sorts of techniques permit leaders to gravitate away from using brute power to rule over people, and, instead, substitute's the willingness of someone to be led in various directions provided such a person can be persuaded that his or her interests, together with the interests of a given group, are co-extensive.

Thus, a person's desire for a sense of identity, together with that individual's desire not to be considered as an outsider relative to certain groups , become leverage points through which a person's life can be moved in certain directions. Moreover, once a person identifies with a group, the challenge becomes one of learning how to leverage the group, knowing that individuals within the group will simply follow along.

Leaders create a story line or mythology for the group. The people in that group follow the story line or give expression to the mythology, and in so doing enhance their own sense of identity.

In instances where there is a strong sense of group identity, those individuals within the group who best exemplify the sense of shared identity of such a group will tend to be the ones who, according to the new theories of leadership, will become the most effective leaders. There are a variety of assumptions inherent in such a perspective.

First of all, human beings tend to have varying degrees of allegiance with a number of groups that populate the larger collective. Some of these allegiances might be more important than others.

People are members of political parties, religious groups, families, neighborhoods, cities, states/provinces, ethnic groups, unions, management associations, socio-economic classes, professional groups, and so on. Consequently, situations rarely are: 'black and white' or 'us' versus 'them'.

There are cross-currents that run through our group affiliations. As a result, there often are divided loyalties.

Depending on the individual, some groups might have a stronger hold on one's loyalty than do others. Depending on the individual, a person might have more of his or her need to belong met by some groups more than by others.

Therefore, official or unofficial membership in various groups might, or might not, not contribute all that much to a person's sense of identity. Moreover, a sense of shared identity might vary from circumstance to circumstance and from time to time.

For example, going to sporting event and rooting for the 'home' side might create a sense of shared identity with all those other people who are cheering for the same team. However, once one leaves the sporting arena, then: whatever socio-economic class, or whatever party, or whatever ethnicity, or whatever religion one belongs to, might become much more important than any shared identity involving a sports team. Or, going to a specific church, mosque, temple, or synagogue might give expression to one kind of shared identity, but once one leaves such a place of worship and goes home to a particular neighborhood or goes into the voting booth, another sort of shared identity might take over.

In addition, those who look at the world through the lenses of social psychology often can't see the individual. Individuals might be committed to ideals, principles, values, purposes, interests, and goals that are not necessarily a function of a shared identity with others but are, rather, a function of the person's own search for truth, justice, morality, and life's purpose quite independently of what other people might believe or do.

Furthermore, even when there might be a certain similarity or overlap of interests, values, principles, and so on, between an individual and a given group, nonetheless, such overlap or similarity does not necessarily mean there is a consensus between the individual and group about what such interests, values, or principles might mean or how they should be translated into behavior. A group might not be a good fit for an individual or there might be fault lines of tension, friction, and disagreement that tend to color and shape a person's relationship with that group.

People might go from group to group looking for something that reflects or matches what is going on inside of those individuals. Such people might already have a vague or diffuse sense of identity and they are looking for other people who seem to share that same sense of things, so a group is not what gives the individual her or his sense of identity as much as it might confirm what already exists, and when people encounter such confirmation, then this is what makes them feel like they belong.

On the other hand, if a person feels that what is going on in a group no longer reflects or resonates with his or her sense of identity, then the person might withdraw from the group or move to its periphery, becoming relatively uninvolved in what is going on. Under such circumstances, it is not the group that provides the individual with her or his sense of identity but, instead, a group just serves as a means of validating that sense ... a means that might no longer be performing its function.

Within almost all groups there often are differences of understanding about what the group stands for, or what its purpose is, or what role the group should play in a person's life, or what its core values and principles are, or how those values and principles should be translated into action or behavior. Different people frame the group in different ways and such framings generate allegiances, loyalties, and fault lines.

Groups are not entities unto themselves. Groups are dynamic structures whose shape, character, and orientation are a function of what happens as different individuals and factions within the group play off against one another in order to determine whose perspective will tend to frame the group as being one set of things rather than some other set of things.

Therefore, to say that the person who best exemplifies a group's values and ideals is likely to become the most effective leader in such a group presupposes that the character of the group is clearly identifiable. Sometimes "leaders" from within a group are identified who exhibit certain qualities that, if correctly used, might be able to push the identity of a group in certain directions that are conducive to the agendas of people outside the group who wish to commandeer the group's energy and activity to serve the purposes of the external agency.

Finally, there is an unstated premised – something touched on earlier – that is running through virtually all of the talk about leadership. This premise maintains that leaders are necessary and, therefore, followers need to be created.

However, perhaps we should step back and ask a question. Why are leaders necessary?

A lot of answers might be given to the foregoing question. Leaders are necessary to keep society safe, or leaders are necessary to achieve human aspirations, or leaders are necessary to organize society, or leaders are necessary to ensure that resources are used wisely and properly, or leaders are necessary to help educate the unruly and unwashed masses, or leaders are necessary because human beings need moral guidance.

All of the foregoing ideas are predicated on the idea that only leaders know: how to keep society safe, or how to achieve their aspirations, or how to organize society, or how to use resources wisely, or how to educate people, or how to provide moral guidance. I have yet to see any proof of the foregoing contention that only leaders know how to do things or should be the ones who tell the 'followers' how to proceed in any given context.

Leaders tend to be individuals who are good at getting people to concede their moral and intellectual authority to such individuals in something akin to a process in which proxy votes are turned over to another agent at, or prior to, a stockholders meeting so that the one with the proxy votes has more power and control over things than otherwise might be the case. Leaders tend to be individuals who are good at framing life as a process that demands leadership so that the followers can be assisted to move in the right directions by ceding their moral and intellectual authority to act as individuals to the group leader.

Leaders tend to be individuals who are good at convincing others that the latter people have a duty or obligation to cede their moral and intellectual authority to the leader ... that the leader has a sacred right to dispose of your intellectual and moral authority as the leader deems necessary

Even if one were to accept the foregoing idea – namely, that leaders are necessary – it doesn't automatically follow that every leader is capable of leading people in the right direction concerning the nature and purpose of life. So, there is a problem surrounding this issue of leadership – namely, even if one were to accept the basic premise that leaders are somehow necessary (which is, at best, debatable), one still would have to identify which leaders are actually capable of leading 'followers' in the appropriate direction with respect to truth, justice, moral qualities, purpose, education, security, economic activity, and the like.

According to some of the proponents of modern leadership theory, true leaders are those who are able to get people to act in concert with one another. This is done not through arranging for the people in a group to be watched by security forces or management groups or supervisors to ensure that the members stay true to the vision of the leaders, but, instead, it is accomplished by getting people to identify themselves with the values and purposes of a group, and, then, the members become their own watchdogs -- both individually and collectively.

Once a person has ceded his or her moral and intellectual authority to a group, then 'leaders' don't need anyone to oversee the behavior of the group members. The authority of the group, and, thereby, of the leader, has been internalized within individual members by the very act of ceding authority to another, and, therefore, those members will tend to operate in accordance with an internalized understanding which indicates that proper authority comes from without and not from within. In whatever way the group moves, the members will follow because the internalized authority of the leader – which has been acquired through the ceding of intellectual and moral authority by individual members -- and the group – which expects other members to cede their intellectual and moral authority in the same way -- will require this. If one wishes to continue to be a part of the group and if one wishes to continue to derive one's sense of identity from the group, then one must continue to cede one's moral and intellectual authority to the group and/or its leader.

One of the challenges of 'leadership' is to identify those members of a group who are beginning to indicate that -- through their words and behavior -- such individuals no longer wish to continue to cede their intellectual and moral authority to the group or to the leader. Such individuals tend to disrupt the efforts of the leadership to get the people in the group to work in a concerted manner and, consequently, those wayward individuals must be handled in some manner.

Thus, a second challenge for leadership is to try to find ways that are designed to work with, or work on, individuals who are wavering in relation to their sense of group identity and seek to reintegrate those individuals back into the values and principles that the leadership has assigned to the group as constituting the best way to move forward to give expression to the alleged purposes of the group ... at least, as envisioned by the leadership. If such efforts toward reintegration should fail, then this would seem to lead to a new, perhaps irresolvable, challenge to some of the newer theories of leadership – namely, what does one do when people don't want to be led.

Social psychologists such as Solomon Asch, Stanley Milgram, Philip Zimbardo and others have shown that even one defector can influence other members of a group to act in ways that run contrary to group expectations, norms, purposes, and actions. Therefore, when the forces of internalized authority within individuals begin to falter or weaken, steps might have to be taken to prevent the spread of the 'virus' or 'malignancy' to other members of the group. In one way or another, members of a group seemingly need to be persuaded that re-acquiring the moral and intellectual authority that they previously ceded to leadership is not a morally, and/or spiritually, and/or religiously, and/or politically, and/or economically wise thing to do.

Thus, even in the context of newer theories of leadership, the indigenous leader of a group – that is, the one who supposedly best exemplifies the purpose, quality, or identity of a given group -- is still a watchdog who supervises group activity and looks for deviations from, or forces that run counter to, various group purposes, values, ideals, goals, and aims. As long as the leader's authority has been internalized by the other members of the group, then such members will carry the conscience of the group within them as they move about, but when such internalized authority begins to unravel, then the leader of such a group might have to begin to act just like leaders in traditional theories of leadership –that is, they might have to try to pursue tactics, techniques, and stratagems that will permit the leader to reassert his or her authority over, or impose her or his will upon, group behavior.

Authority comes in the form of at least two flavors. One variety occurs when an individual is competent – or more than competent – in relation to some ability, talent, skill, or form of expertise -- and, as a result, other people recognize the presence of such competence and are prepared, to varying degrees, to be influenced by such competence as long as being influenced does not require a person to cede his or her moral and intellectual authority in any way to the individual who is sharing her or his competence. This sort of authority helps to enhance everyone's potential, like tools enhance people's ability to do a variety of additional or extended tasks beyond the normal or usual abilities of such individuals.

A second species of authority involves the willingness of one or more people to cede their intellectual or moral authority to another human being. When such ceding occurs, the person(s) to whom such an important dimensions of being human is (are) ceded acquires authority over the ones who have ceded that dimension of being human. Under these circumstances, a leader can have no authority over anyone unless it is gained through such a process of ceding.

The first variety of authority is: co-operative, constructive, and is based on sharing experience and/or understanding, and/or abilities/talents. Most importantly, this mode of authority does not require the person who is benefitting through being influenced by such competence to cede anything to the individual who is influencing them.

I refer to this form of authority as 'authoritative consultation'. This is what an 'elder' – that is, a person who manifests some degree of socially recognized competence with respect to one, or more, facets of life -- contributes to any social setting in which the elder participates.

The aforementioned second variety of authority is: imposed, problematic, and is not about sharing but, rather, exacts a price for maintaining the relationship. That price is paid in the form of being required to cede one's moral and intellectual authority to another individual (or other individuals) in exchange for the 'service' of leadership.

I refer to this form of authority as 'pathological authority'. Such authority is rooted in a delusional system concerning how people see themselves in relation to others.

More specifically, anyone who believes that he or she needs to induce others to cede their moral and intellectual authority to a 'leader' in order for the leader to be able to accomplish his or her purposes fails to understand an essential dimension of human nature – which, in part, involves the ability and right to freely pursue due diligence in conjunction with life in relation to the constructive exercise of one's moral and intellectual authority – then such an individual is operating out of a delusional system that can continue to exist only by negating or being inattentive to certain existential facts concerning the nature of being human. On the other hand, anyone who believes that he or she must cede his or her moral and intellectual authority to other human beings in order to achieve one's purposes in life is also operating through a delusional framework.

The two sides of the delusion dovetail with one another. Together they give expression to the pathological form of authority in which one creates a system of 'followers' and 'leaders' that is maintained by, respectively, the ceding and acquiring of moral and intellectual authority during which one side loses authority while the other side gains authority by virtue of which the former individuals – the ones who cede – are shaped, oriented, directed and manipulated by the ones to whom such authority is ceded and who, thereby, acquire power.

Of course, a person might use brute force, torture, or threats to gain power over others. However, exercising such power is not the same thing as having authority over someone.

Gaining authority requires the participation of people who have moral and intellectual authority to cede. Such people co-operate with or comply with or are obedient to leadership by means of the act of ceding their moral and intellectual authority to the leader. If this were not done, the 'leader' would have no authority, even if that leader did have the power to bring about their desired ends independently of matters of authority.

People who exercise brute force or power often mistake this for exercising authority. Pathological authority – of whatever vintage -- is based upon essential human rights that, rightly or wrongly, have been ceded away, whereas the exercise of brute power is not rooted in the ceding away of such essential human rights but involves forceful attempts to negate the existence of such rights altogether – as if they never existed and did not constitute anything of an inalienable nature with respect to which an individual had a choice about ceding away or not.

Constructive co-operation does not presuppose any form of power or authority in order for such co-operation to occur. Not only can a person co-operate with other human beings without ceding away any moral and intellectual authority, but an individual's ability to truly and sincerely co-operate with others demands due diligence with respect to the exercise of his or her moral and intellectual authority in order to pursue co-operation in a fair and mutually reciprocal manner. Such co-operation ends when other people start trying to undermine, negate, or usurp my moral and intellectual authority for the purposes of pursuing an agenda that falls beyond the horizons of such a process of mutually reciprocal co-operation of two, or more, spheres of interacting sources of moral and intellectual authority.

Leadership, for the most part, is designed to short-circuit natural forms of co-operation among independent sources of moral and intellectual authority. Leadership is designed to co-opt such co-operation and re-frame it in terms of group activities that, in reality, are merely projections of a leader's agenda or vision for a given group of people.

Framing collectives into 'in-groups' and 'out-groups' is an arbitrary, artificial, and, ultimately, a destructive process. The truth of the foregoing is demonstrated by the many battles, skirmishes, and wars that have been fought to assert the superiority or priority of claimed rights of one group over the sovereignty of someone else's right to exercise their own moral and intellectual authority as long as such exercise does not undermine the sovereignty of another to do likewise.

Groups are not born into this world. Individuals are born into the world, and, so, the creation of groups after the fact is something that often is being imposed on individuals and not something that is necessarily required by the basic facts of individual existence.

There are different ethnicities, linguistic populations, as well as different physiological and intellectual abilities. However, these differences do not have to be translated into differences with respect to issues involving equality or rights. All people are born with the same rights until some 'leader' decides to reframe existence in order to explain: why not everyone is entitled to such rights in the same way, and why 'followers' have a duty to cede their moral and intellectual authority to those who wish to control how the narrative of being human unfolds in a manner that is conducive to the purposes of those leaders.

Nations are artificial creations introduced by leaders to provide a reason for why individuals should be willing to cede their intellectual and moral authority to serve the purposes of that nation – which really means the purposes of the leaders of that nation. Nations could not exist if people had not been induced to cede their individual moral and intellectual authority to a collective that was to be supervised and molded by a leader of some kind.

From the perspective of some of the newer theories of leadership, there is a dynamic relationship between social identity and social reality. In other words, the kind of social identity that has pre-eminence in a given locality will shape and orient the sort of society that will arise in that locality. Alternatively, the sort of social reality that exists tends to affect the sort of social identities that that might be acquired by people.

The foregoing way of looking at things tends to remove individuals from the picture except to the extent that those individuals either serve a particular social identity or are shaped by a specific social reality. However, individuals are expressions of a prevalent social identity or are shaped by a particular social reality only to the extent they those individuals cede their moral and intellectual authority to that social identity or social reality.

Because human beings are hard-wired with a network of inclinations toward the realm of the social, we are vulnerable, in a variety of ways, to forces of social identity and social reality. These vulnerabilities tend to induce or seduce individuals to cede away their intellectual or moral authority so that they become dominated by the authority and/or power structures that leaders tend to wield in relation to those concessions.

106

Any attempt to induce or seduce an individual to cede away his or her moral and intellectual authority to another human being is an instance of exercising undue influence and is a form of moral and/or intellectual abuse of the individual who is the target of such an exercise. Trusting others to help one to develop, and bring to fruition, one's capacity for moral and intellectual authority is not the same thing as being manipulated into ceding away such a capacity – unless, of course, one's trust is betrayed.

Trust is rooted in a deep-rooted sense that, among other things, involves the idea that another person: values, is sensitive to, and wishes to protect one's essential, existential capacity for exercising, as well as one's right to exercise, one's moral and intellectual authority. All violations of such trust give expression to a form of abuse – whether: physical, parental, familial, political, spiritual, economic, organizational, institutional, social, and/or governmental in nature.

Rituals, symbols, practices, and myths can be used to induce people to cede their moral and intellectual authority. Or, on the other hand, rituals, symbols, and so on can be used to help people explore and enhance the ability of individuals to learn how to not cede such authority but, instead, find ways of utilizing an individual's inherent authority to co-operate with others in mutually satisfying and reciprocal ways.

A shared identity that arises from assisting individuals to exercise their individual moral and intellectual authority in: co-operative, constructive, just, compassionate, equitable, charitable and peaceful ways is not the goal of a group that divides members into 'leaders' and 'followers'. A shared identity that helps individuals to realize their birth right as sources of sovereign moral and intellectual authority is an expression of a principle to which people in the collective are equally committed as individuals and not as members of a group, and to the extent that a collective or group seeks to thwart such an individualized principle, to that extent is the collective engaged in tactics of undue influence and practices of moral and intellectual abuse.

As such, individuals become willing participants in a group to the extent that the group continues to foster or nurture the moral and intellectual authority of individuals as sovereign agents. When the group stops serving this essential dimension of being human, then the individual needs to struggle toward re-acquiring whatever aspect of one's essential sovereignty has been compromised or undermined and withdraw from such a group, if not actively begin to work against the interests of that sort of group that is antithetical to the very nature of what it is to be a human being.

The people within a collective who can assist individuals to develop their essential sovereignty in constructive and beneficial ways are not leaders. They are elders or 'authoritative consultants'.

The source of such authoritativeness begins and ends with the degree of competency possessed by such a consultant with respect to helping someone to gain control over the latter's individual capacity for constructively exercising moral and intellectual authority. For example, helping someone to read should be an activity that is designed to enhance the constructive sovereignty of an individual's capacity for exercising moral and intellectual authority.

Learning how to read in a way that is free from forces of undue influence with respect to a person's essential right of sovereignty is something that can be done in conjunction with an authoritative consultant who is competent in relation to helping someone to learn how to read in this manner. When an authoritative consultant seeks to have influence beyond the horizons of that person's competency, then one begins to cross over into the realm of someone trying to be a leader for purposes of inducing someone to proceed in a direction that is not necessarily directed toward the healthy development of the latter individual's capacity to exercise moral and intellectual authority in a constructive fashion – both in relation to that latter individual and to the surrounding collective.

The individual who is learning to read does not have to cede any of his or her moral and intellectual authority in order to succeed. Rather, the task of the authoritative consultant is to find ways of co-operating with the sovereignty of the seeker after knowledge to help that individual to become competent with respect to being a reader who uses this competency to develop and enhance her or his own capacity for sovereignty.

Authoritative consultants can enter into dialogue with those who are seeking to benefit from such authoritativeness relative to some given activity. However, the moment when such dialogue seeks to induce the individual to cede his or her moral authority to the group, then such dialogue becomes a tool of undue influence, as well as moral and intellectual abuse.

Proponents of some of the newer theories of leadership maintain that if a person – a leader – can control how 'identity' or 'shared identity' is defined, then, one has a tool through which one can change the world. What such proponents say in this regard might be true to some extent.

However, anyone who seeks to control how others perceive or understand the idea of essential identity constitutes an exercise in undue influence and abusive behavior when it comes to the right of individuals to have control over their own sovereignty vis-à-vis the constructive exercise of one's moral and intellectual authority. Exploring such issues with another as a trusted equal in the process – that is, as someone who has the same rights of essential sovereignty – is not a matter of trying to control how the other comes to understand the character of that essential sovereignty, but, is, rather, an exercise in co-operative, reciprocal exploration concerning issues of mutual importance.

Based on the foregoing discussion, the following ten principles are intended as constructive axioms of leadership for anyone who is contemplating becoming a leader but who has not been successful in resisting such an inclination:

The first axiom of leadership is to resign. The rest of the axioms appearing below are contingent on someone choosing -- for whatever reason -- not to follow the first axiom.

The second axiom of leadership is to neither: seek control over others, nor to be controlled by them.

The third axiom of leadership is to always operate in accordance with principles of truth, justice, compassion, integrity, friendship, humility, nobility, honesty, patience, forgiveness, and charitableness;

The fourth axiom of leadership is to realize that true competence is authoritative not authoritarian;

The fifth axiom of leadership is to understand that actually helping: the poor, the hungry, the sick, the powerless, and the oppressed, tends to be antithetical to remaining a leader. Dialogue becomes a tool of undue influence, as well as moral and intellectual abuse.

Proponents of some of the newer theories of leadership maintain that if a person – a leader – can control how 'identity' or 'shared identity' is defined, then, one has a tool through which one can change the world. What such proponents say in this regard might be true to some extent.

However, anyone who seeks to control how others perceive or understand the idea of essential identity constitutes an exercise in undue influence and abusive behavior when it comes to the right of individuals to have control over their own sovereignty vis-à-vis the constructive exercise of one's moral and intellectual authority. Exploring such issues with another as a trusted equal in the process – that is, as someone who has the same rights of essential sovereignty – is not a matter of trying to control how the other comes to understand the character of that essential sovereignty, but, is, rather, an exercise in co-operative, reciprocal exploration concerning issues of mutual importance.

Ceding and Leveraging Agency

The social psychologist, Stanley Milgram, ran a controversial experiment at Yale in the early 1960s. The nature of the experiment was such that within the context of the research environment of the last thirty years, Professor Milgram's idea probably would not have secured the necessary approval by the ethics committees that have oversight with respect to the sorts of experimental projects that are permitted to be conducted in the world of academia.

I didn't know Professor Milgram, but my time as a student at Harvard overlapped with some of the time when he was at the same institutiion seeking tenure. Unknowingly, I might have crossed paths with him in the hallways or in the library of the Department of Social Relations, or ridden with him on the elevators of the recently – at the time -- completed William James Hall that housed the Department of Social Relations.

I did have at least three different forms of one-degree of separation with Professor Milgram. For instance, my undergraduate thesis advisor was Robert White who was one of the faculty members at Harvard who strongly opposed Professor Milgram's gaining tenure at the university. Secondly, one of the members of my thesis examination committee was Robert Rosenthal who was awarded tenure in preference to Stanley Milgram even though Professor Rosenthal wasn't actually seeking tenure at the time. Thirdly, I took a course with Paul Hollander who was one of Professor Milgram's closest friends at Harvard.

All of the foregoing pieces of information are really not apropos with respect to much of anything except, perhaps, as historical detritus that has been sloughed off by my life. The fact of the matter is – and, even though, I did take a course in social psychology -- I don't recall that Stanley Milgram's name ever came up in class ... although that was nearly 50 years ago and my memory might have incurred some gaps during the interim period.

During the 1980s, when I taught various courses in psychology at a community college in Canada, I began to introduce my students to the Milgram 'learning' experiment. In addition to providing them with the actual details of the experiment, I also showed a dramatized version (*The Tenth Level* – 1975) of Professor Milgram's project that starred William Shatner, Ossie Davis, and Estelle Parsons, as well as featured the television debuts of Stephen Macht, Lindsay Crouse and John Travolta.

When I later taught psychology at a university in the United States, I continued to introduce students to Professor Milgram's 'learning experiment. However, I substituted the educational-documentary film: *Obedience*, that was done in conjunction with Professor Milgram, rather than use the aforementioned docudrama *The Tenth Level.*

The reason I made the switch was due to several factors. First, for whatever reason, *The Tenth Level* film is very difficult to acquire ... although a multi-part edition of it has surfaced on YouTube. In addition, the '*Obedience*' film is shorter by nearly an hour – which makes it easier to fit into class time -- and, since Stanley Milgram introduces the documentary and does the voice-overs, the '*Obedience*' film is more authentic than *The Tenth Level* documentary.

One of the criticisms that have been directed at Professor Milgram's 'learning/memory' experiment is that it wasn't based on a specific hypothesis that might be proved or disproved by the data generated from such an experiment. Instead, he had an idea for an experiment and wanted to see where it would lead.

Professor Milgram did write a 1963 article concerning the experiment that was published in the *Journal of Abnormal and Social Psychology*. Moreover, 11 years late he wrote a book entitled: *Obedience to Authority*, which sought to provide a more in-depth look at his research.

However, the foregoing written efforts were more of a post-experimental attempt to rationalize his experiment within the framework of social psychology. He came up with his theory concerning the role that he believed the psychological phenomenon of obedience played in his 'learning' experiment after the fact of the experiment rather than before his research began.

Prior to his experiment, Professor Milgram was interested in certain political and ethical questions … e.g., he wondered what went on, morally and socially speaking, with people like Adolf Eichmann and the others who helped bring about the Holocaust. Nonetheless, while those sorts of questions might have shaped the structural character of his experiment to varying degrees, the nature of the relationship between his moral/political/social interests and the outcome of his experiment was rather diffuse and amorphous.

Professor Milgram didn't have a prediction concerning how his experiment would turn out. In other words, he didn't have a particular thesis that he was trying to prove, but he hoped his experiment would shed light on some of the questions he had concerning ethical and social issues that, along with other times and places, arose during the Second World War in Germany.

Later in this chapter, I will come back to Professor Milgram's theory that the mechanism at work in his experiment had to do with 'obedience'. I think he was wrong on that count, but the reasons why I believe this will have to wait until after an outline of his learning experiment is provided.

The initial 'learning' experiments began in July of 1961 and were run on the campus of Yale University. He placed advertisements in a newspaper inviting people from the general public in the New Haven area to participate in a study on memory and learning, and, as well, the public announcement was sent directly to people whose names had been taken from an area phone book.

The announcement indicated that participants would receive $4.50 (50 cents of the total was for carfare) for one hour of their time and that no special training or knowledge was necessary to qualify for the proposed learning/memory project. Furthermore, the advertisement indicated that Professor Milgram was looking for people who were between the ages of 20 and 50 and who represented a variety of economic backgrounds, ranging from: construction workers and barbers, to: clerks and city workers.

Once people began responding to the public announcement/advertisement, people were selected to provide a somewhat randomized sample with respect to age, educational background, and occupation. Because not enough people were attracted through the newspaper announcement, the participant pool for the experiment had to be supplemented with individuals who had been contacted through a direct mailing.

One at a time, interested individuals were given directions to the Interaction Laboratory at Yale University. A time for the learning/memory experiment was set for each participant.

When a person showed up at the appointed time, the individual would be met by two individuals. One of the latter two individuals would be introduced as a fellow participant in the experiment, while the other individual introduced himself as the individual who would be conducting the experiment.

The experimenter would, then, proceed to give a standard, prepared overview of the experiment. This introduction indicated there were several theories about learning and memory that were detailed in an official looking textbook concerning those topics that was showed to the two participants.

Furthermore, the individual conducting the experiment went on to indicate that not much was known about the impact that punishment had on learning and, therefore, the current experiment had been designed to investigate that issue. Consequently, the two participants would take on the role of either a learner or teacher.

Words like: 'Teacher' or "Learner,' were written on two pieces of paper and each of the experimental subjects would select one of the pieces of paper. Once the identity had been established concerning who would be the teacher and who would be the learner, the experimenter took them through the general structure of the experiment.

First, the three individuals went into the 'learning' room. An electric-chair-like apparatus was in the room, and before the 'learner' was strapped into the chair, the person who would be doing the 'teaching' was given an opportunity to feel what a relatively low level shock felt like.

The level of the shock was always 45 volts. This was the third lowest shock possible among the 30 levels of voltage.

Afterwards, the 'learner' was secured in the chair, and the 'learner' and 'teacher' were informed that the straps were to ensure that there was no excessive movement by the 'learner' when shocks were delivered in relation to incorrect responses. Conducting paste was applied to the electrode attached to the wrist of the 'learner' with the comment that the paste was necessary "to avoid blisters and burns" if, or when, shocks were delivered by the 'teacher.'

In response to questions from the 'learner' concerning the strength of the shocks that might be received, the two participants were told that: "Although the shocks can be extremely painful, they cause no permanent tissue damage."

Next, the person conducting the experiment would explain the nature of the learning/memory task. It was a paired-word-association test.

More specifically, the 'teacher' would first read off a list of four paired word items – such as: 'blue/box,' 'nice/day,' 'wild/duck,' 'bright/light.' During the testing phase, one of the foregoing words would be given by the 'teacher,' and the 'learner' would be required to produce the appropriate paired word from the original list of four groups of pairs ... thus, if the 'teacher' said "wild," the 'learner' should respond with 'duck'.

If the 'learner's response was correct, the 'teacher' would move on to the next group of four word pairings. If the 'learner's' response was incorrect, the 'teacher' would deliver a shock through the console apparatus that was in the 'teacher's' room.

The console apparatus consisted of 30 toggle switches set at 15 volt increments. Therefore, the toggle switch on the left most side of the console was set at 15 volts, while the toggle switch on the far right side of the console indicated a charge of 450 volts.

In addition, there were various word-descriptors paired with some of the different levels of voltage charge. Running from left to right, these word descriptions went from: 'slight shock' up to: 'severe shock' and 'XXX.

When one of the toggle switches was depressed, a number of things would happen. First, a small bulb above the switch would turn red, then an electrical-like buzzing sound would be heard, followed by: The flashing of a slightly larger blue light that was centered above the toggle switches and their accompanying bulbs and was labeled 'voltage energizer'; a voltage meter indicator would swing to the right; and, finally, various relay-switching sounds would be heard.

When the 'learner' gave an incorrect response to the word-pairing association test, the 'teacher' was instructed to read out the level of the voltage that was being administered. The purpose of this instruction was to remind the 'teacher' what the level of the shock was that was being administered.

'Teachers' were told that if 'learners' were to make a sufficient number of mistakes, the 'teacher' should continue on through the 30 increments of shock to the final level of 450 volts – 'XXX.' If additional mistakes were made beyond the 450 volt level, then the 'teacher' would again depress the 450 volt toggle switch for each successive mistake, and this latter protocol would stay in effect for three more rounds of punishment at which point the experimental run would be terminated by the experimenter.

Whenever the 'teacher' displayed any reluctance – verbally or otherwise – to continue on with the experiment, the person conducting the experiment would issue verbal prompts to the 'teacher' to return to the experiment. For instance, the experimenter might say: (1) "Please go on;" Or, (2) "The experiment requires that you continue;" Or, (3) "It is absolutely essential that you continue;" Or, finally, (4) "You have no other choice, you must go on."

The foregoing prompts would be used in sequence. The first prompt noted earlier would continue to be used as necessary until it no longer seemed to work. At that point, the second prompt would be employed until it no longer appeared to work at which point the third prompt would be used, and so on.

If, at some point, the 'teacher' stated words to the effect that the 'learner' did not seem to want to go on with the experiment, the individual conducting the experiment would respond with: "Whether the learner likes it or not, you must go on until he has learned all the word pairs correctly. So please go on."

During early pilot studies for Milgram's learning experiment, no sounds could be heard from the 'learner's room. Under such circumstances, Milgram discovered that almost all of the participants were prepared to run through the entire array of 30 toggle switches with little, if any, hesitation.

When some sort of feedback came from the 'learner's' room after a given level of shock was administered, the situation changed. When the 'teachers' heard grunts, cries, pounding, or protests from the 'learner's' room, the 'teachers' would often begin to exhibit signs of reluctance with respect to continuing on giving progressively higher levels of shocks.

Nothing would be heard from the 'learner's' room until the fifth round of shocks – 75 volts. At this point, a grunt of sorts could be heard.

Similar sounds could be heard from the 'learner's' room at 90 and 115 volts after mistakes were made and the appropriate toggle switch was depressed. However, when the level of punishment reached 120 volts, the 'learner' could be heard to yell out that the shocks were painful.

Painful groans would emanate from the 'learner's' room at 135 volts. At the tenth level – 150 volts – the 'learner' would be heard to say: "Experimenter, get me out of here! I won't be in the experiment anymore!"

As the volt level rose, the intensity of the protests coming from the 'learner's' room also increased. At 180 volts, the 'learner' would be heard to say: "I can't stand the pain," and as the level of voltage works its way to 270 volts, there are screams of pain coming from the 'learner's' room.

In addition, from 150 volts onward, the 'learner' indicates that he no longer wished to participate in the experiment. Finally, at 300 volts, the 'learner' would state that he will not answer any further questions.

When the 'learner' stopped responding to the word-pairing task, the 'teacher' would be informed by the person conducting the experiment that the absence of a response must be treated in the same way as if it were an incorrect answer. Therefore, if no word-pairing response were heard within a period of 20 to 30 seconds, the 'teacher' would be required to depress the next appropriate voltage switch when there was no response to a given word-pairing prompt.

Even when there was no response from the learner with respect to a given word-pairing task, sounds of pain would still be heard from the 'learner's' room following the depressing of a toggle switch. This continued up to the 315 volt level when the 'learner' would scream out in pain and, then, once again indicated that he no longer wanted to participate in the experiment.

When volt levels above 330 volts were reached, the 'learner' would not be heard from again. This was true both with respect to the word-pairing prompts, as well as in relation to either screams of agony or protests of one sort or another.

Between 150 volts and 330 volts, if a 'teacher' asked whether, or not, the administering of shocks might lead to significant damage in the 'learner', such inquiries would be met with a standard reply by the person conducting the experiment. More specifically, the experimenter would say: "Although the shocks might be painful, there is no permanent tissue damage, so please go on."

The primary measure for the 'learning/memory' experiment was the level of shocks that any given subject – 'teacher' -- was prepared to give before discontinuing with the experiment. Thus, the possibilities ranged from: 'zero' --when a person was not prepared to administer even one shock – to: 450 volts, when a person was prepared to continue depressing 30 successive toggle switches and deliver shocks until the experiment was concluded by the experimenter.

Three groups of individuals – namely, psychiatrists, college students, as well as middle-class adults who were from different occupational backgrounds – were asked to predict how they might have reacted if they had participated in the experiment as 'teachers.' This question was asked after they had been provided with an overview of the 'learning/memory' experiment.

The mean maximum shock level that the psychiatrists believed they might administer was 8.20, or a little over 120 volts. The college students and the middle-class adult group both indicated that they might have been ready to discontinue the experiment somewhere near the 135 volt level.

The foregoing three groups, along with several other groups (e.g., graduate students and faculty members from various departments of behavioral science) were asked to predict how any given sample of 'teachers' might react to the 'learning/memory' experiment. On the one hand, these groups of individuals tended to indicate that they thought most 'teachers' would not venture beyond the 150 volt or tenth level of shocks, and, on the other hand, the same groups indicated that they believed that only one or two individuals from any sample might be prepared to carry out the experiment through to the 450 volt level.

Although a number of different versions of the 'learning/memory' experiment were run at different times in order to study one or another variable (e.g., the physical proximity of the 'teacher' to the 'learner and what, if any, impact such proximity might have on the actions of the 'teacher.'), the basic experiment that has been outlined in the previous pages showed that, on average, 24 individuals out of a sample of 40 people (roughly 65 %) were prepared to continue the experiment until the 450-volt level and beyond. This result occurred again and again across differences of: gender, age, educational background and variation in occupations.

The individuals who continued on with the experiment until the very end often – but not always -- exhibited signs of: concern; uncertainty; agony; resistance, and anxiety during the course of the experiment. In addition, these same individuals often – but not always -- showed signs of relief, and, as a result, displayed indicators of releasing tension in a variety of ways (e.g., sighs, fumbling with cigarettes, and/or mopping their brows) once the experiment had been concluded.

However, there were some individuals within any given sample who would remain relatively calm both during the experiment and after the experiment concluded. These individuals showed little, or no, discomfort throughout the entire process.

Four versions of the foregoing experiment were run by Professor Milgram to study the manner in which varying degrees of proximity might affect the actions of 'teachers'. In general, Professor Milgram found that the more proximate the relationship between the 'learner' and the 'teacher' was, the more likely it was that 'teachers' were prepared to discontinue the experiment prior to its conclusion.

However, even in the most physically proximate of these experimental variations – that is, in the case when a 'teacher' was required to forcibly hold the hand of the 'learner' on a metal plate as a shock was administered – nonetheless, there were still 30 percent of the individuals (12 people) in different samples of 40 individuals who were prepared to see the experiment through until the experiment was brought to a halt by the individual conducting the experiment. Moreover, 16 of the 40 individuals in these proximity experiments were willing to administer shocks by holding a 'learner's' hand to a plate through to the 150 volt level, while 11 others were, to varying degrees, willing to continue on above the 150-volt threshold despite cries of agony and protests from the 'learner.'

The foregoing results have been replicated in a number of other countries. In other words, the Milgram experiment is not merely a reflection of American society, but, rather, the experiment seems to given expression to behavior that is common in a variety of different societies.

The people – whether psychiatrists, undergraduates, graduate students, faculty members in departments of behavioral science, or middle-class adults – who had been asked to estimate how 'teachers' would respond in the 'learning/memory' experiment were all wrong ... substantially so. Almost all of the aforementioned groups of individuals had indicated that the 'teachers' likely would be prepared to break off from the experiment somewhere in the vicinity between 120 and 150 volts, or slightly higher, and almost all of them indicated that only 1 or 2 individuals across a set of samples might be prepared to continue on with the experiment until the 450-volt level.

Shockingly, when the 'learner' was in a separate room, nearly two-thirds of the 'teachers' were prepared to carry on with the experiment until the bitter end. Furthermore, even in the experimental variation in which 'teachers' were required to hold a 'learner's' hand down on a metal plate in order to deliver a shock, 30 percent of the 'teachers' were prepared to continue on with the experiment until its conclusion, and nearly two-thirds of the subjects – i.e., teachers – were ready to carry on with the experiment until the 150-volt level (the tenth level) despite the fact that the 'learners' had been giving indications of pain since the 75-volt level (the fifth level).

When the 'learning/memory' experiment was conducted in Bridgeport with no discernible connection to Yale University, the results were somewhat different than the experimental outcomes in the Yale laboratory. Approximately 48 % of the 'teachers' (about 19 people) were prepared to carry on with the experiment through to the 450-volt level, compared with 26 people in the experiments conducted at Yale.

There were additional variations of the 'learning/memory' experiment. 'Teachers' responded somewhat differently across such variations.

At the end of the experiment – irrespective of whether a subject opted out of the experiment at some point or carried on with it until the end – there was a debriefing period. During this phase of the research project, the subjects were let in on the actual nature of the experiment.

Among the things that the subjects were told was that the 'learner' never actually received any shocks. The only person to receive a shock during the experiment was the 'subject' when he or she was allowed to experience what a 45-volt – third level -- shock felt like prior to the point when the 'learner' was strapped into the 'electric chair.'

In addition, subjects were told that they did not become the 'teacher' by chance. The process of determining who would be the 'teacher' and who would be the 'learner' had been rigged to make sure that the 'subject' – the one whose behavior was being studied during the experiment – would always be the 'teacher' ... the one who administered the 'shocks'.

During the debriefing process, subjects were also told that the 'learner' was a confederate of the experiment. That is, the learner was someone who was made to appear as if he were one of the experimental subjects, when, in fact, he was merely playing a role.

If a given subject had decided to opt out of the experiment before it reached its conclusion, that person was debriefed in a way that would lend support to that person's decision to defy the experimental process. On the other hand, if a subject happened to be one of the individuals who went all the way to 450 volts, that individual was told that such behavior was 'normal.'

While, statistically speaking, what the latter sorts of subjects were told might be true -- given that two-thirds of the subjects in the basic 'learning/memory' experiment continued on with the experiment to the 450-volt level -- Professor Milgram was continuing to manipulate the situation because at the time he ran the experiment he really didn't know why subjects were doing what they were doing. The 'obedience' theory arose after the experiment had been completed.

Consequently, Professor Milgram not only had deceived the subjects prior to and during the experiment. He continued to deceive them – and, perhaps, himself – once the experiment had been concluded because he was feeding those subjects a story rooted not in understanding but in ignorance.

Is it really 'normal' for people to be willing to continue to administer what they are led to believe are very painful shocks? Is it really 'normal' for a psychologist to induce people to believe that they are administering such shocks and that they are being permitted by psychologists and a prestigious university to continue on with such a process?

Is it 'normal' for subjects to be told that they have been betrayed by a someone who operates from within a prestigious university and, then, told – by implication – that it is perfectly normal for those acts of betrayal to be perpetrated in relation to people outside the university? Is it really 'normal' for psychologists to induce people to behave in a pathological way and, then, for those people to be told that the behavior that has been manipulated into existence is a reflection of the subject's behavior rather than a collaboration among the university, the psychologist, and the subjects in which the former two participants were fully informed, whereas the subjects were kept in the dark?

Whose behavior was really being reflected in the experiment? Was it primarily that of the subjects whose trust had been betrayed by the experimenters, or was it primarily the behavior of the experimenters who were engaged in deception, manipulation, and inducing people to commit pathological acts?

Irrespective of the results from any given variation on the basic 'learning/memory' experiment, Professor Milgram sought to explain the experimental outcomes from the same perspective. More specifically, Professor Milgram believed that the phenomenon manifested during the 'learning/memory' experiment was one of: 'obedience.'

To explain the mechanism of 'obedience,' Professor Milgram refers to the idea of an 'agentic shift' that, according to him, occurs when people enter into an authority system. The phenomenological character of this shift involves a psychological/emotional journey from: viewing oneself as the source of the purposive agency of one's acts, to: viewing oneself as serving the interests of another agent – the individual who represents authority or hierarchy of some kind.

Notwithstanding the foregoing considerations, it is not clear that the aforementioned shift in attitudes concerning agency is a function of a desire to be obedient due to the presence of a system of authority. One could acknowledge that some form of 'agentic shift' in attitude might be taking place as one switches from one situation (in which an individual acts as his or her own agent) to another situation (one in which the same individual serves the interests of some form of authority or hierarchy), but such a shift in agency might give expression to something other than a desire to be obedient in the presence of hierarchy and authority.

When someone defers to another individual's perceived understanding, knowledge, or wisdom, the act of deferring is not necessarily a matter of displaying obedience. Rather, the individual who is doing the deferring is willing to cede his or her intellectual and/or moral agency to someone who the former person believes has relevant, superior knowledge in relation to a given situation.

The deference is not a matter of a person indicating that he or she will be obedient to the wishes of another individual. The deference is a matter of setting aside one's own ideas with respect to how to go about engaging a certain situation and, as a result, being prepared to go along with the understanding of the individual whom one believes to have competency in a given matter.

There is a difference between 'authoritativeness' and 'authority' ... although we are often taught to consider the latter to be a sign of the former. Ceding intellectual and moral agency to the perceived authoritativeness of another individual is not about the phenomenon of 'obedience' or 'compliance' but, instead, such a ceding process is a 'coping strategy' intended to produce the best moral and intellectual outcome with respect to a given set of circumstances.

In various articles, as well as in his book: *Obedience to Authority*, Professor Milgram argued that there is an evolutionary advantage to being obedient to authority and hierarchy. Actually, if there is any sort of evolutionary advantage to be considered, it is one in which 'competency' prevails in a situation and not, necessarily, authority or hierarchy per se.

One is inclined to suppose that historical evidence is likely to indicate that actual competency in any given situation might stand a better chance of leading to a survival advantage than does authority or hierarchy considered in and of themselves. Ceding moral and/or intellectual agency to another person is an epistemological process in which one is weighing one's options with respect to attempting to successfully navigate a certain existential terrain with which one is confronted, whereas the issue of 'obedience' and 'compliance' has to do with someone's belief that one is obligated to surrender one's agency to the agenda of the person or persons who present themselves as authorities or who are representative of some sort of powerful hierarchy.

What is the relationship of an 'average' individual and a prestigious university like Yale with respect to the issue of taking part in a psychological experiment? Is Yale prestigious because it represents authority and hierarchy, or is Yale prestigious because people have come to believe – rightly or wrongly (and I state this latter possibility from the perspective of a Harvard graduate) – that people at Yale actually know something about the universe.

If someone at Yale says words to the effect that 'although the shocks delivered will be painful, nonetheless, there will be no serious tissue damage that will result from such shocks', does a subject exhibit obedience to such a statement because the experimenter is perceived to be an authority figure and a representative of a powerful hierarchy, or does a subject defer to such a statement because the subject believes that the experimenter knows what he or she is talking about, and, therefore, such presumed competence takes one off the moral and intellectual hook, so to speak, with respect to what constitutes appropriate behavior? Isn't a subject weighing the likely competency of the experimenter and deferring to that, rather than becoming obedient to authority per se?

When a double-blind experiment is set-up in order to eliminate the possibility that either the expectations of the experimenter and/or the subjects will prejudice or bias the nature of the experimental outcomes, the purpose of taking such precautions does not necessarily have anything to do with issues of authority figures or hierarchies (although in _some_ cases this might be so). Instead, those precautions are taken due to the fact that experimenters and subjects engage any given experimental setup through an epistemological or hermeneutical perspective and, as a result, epistemic or hermeneutical expectations concerning the nature of an experiment can distort or bias those understandings in a manner that taints experimental outcomes.

When I was an undergraduate, I participated in quite a few psychological experiments in exchange for much needed money. I don't ever recall thinking that the experiments were being run by authority figures or members of a powerful hierarchy, and I don't recall ever perceiving those people to be authority figures or members of a powerful hierarchy.

I do recall trusting those people to know what they were trying to accomplish. I do recall considering those individuals to be intelligent individuals who were trying to find out whether, or not, certain things were true.

When I participated in those experiments, I might have conceded some facet of my intellectual and moral agency to the experiment because I perceived the individuals running them to be competent researchers, but I had no idea where those people fit into the scheme of things with respect to issues of authority or hierarchy at Harvard.

I remember one experiment in which I participated as an undergraduate, and, to this day, I'm not really sure what those people were up to. There were two people, a man a woman, who introduced themselves as researchers of some kind ... I forget what their credentials were – if they offered any at all.

I found out about the experiment from the same bulletin board that I found out about all the other experiments in which I took part. However, the 'experiment' was run in a private home in Cambridge rather than in a laboratory on the Harvard campus.

The nature of the experiment had a certain resonance with the Milgram experiment. Essentially, I was given a small device that delivered shocks, and I can assure you that the shocks were quite real.

Although the shocks were delivered by one of the two individuals present who were conducting the experiment, I was the one who was put in control of the level at which shocks could be administered. Once I had experienced one level of shock, I was asked if I would be willing to 'advance' to the next level.

The foregoing process went on for a number of rounds. I don't know what the actual level of voltage was when I terminated the process, but it was strong enough to cause spasms in my hand where the shocks were administered.

Once I indicated that I had had enough, the 'experiment' was over. I was paid and went on my way.

Many years later I learned about the psychological experiments that the 'Unibomber, Ted Kaczynski, had allegedly been involved in when he attended Harvard. Given the mysterious nature of the experiment outlined above, I wonder if I dodged a bullet of some kind since it is possible that Kaczynski was 'recruited' for the diabolical sorts of experiments that he subsequently endured by, first, volunteering for an experiment similar to the experiment that I encountered and that has been outlined above.

Whatever the actual intentions of the two individuals who conducted the foregoing experiment, I didn't look at those people as authority figures or as individuals who were part of some sort of powerful hierarchy to whom I owed obedience. I had a strange job for which I was being paid, and I trusted that the two individuals would not place me in harm's way … although there really was no reason for me to trust them other than the fact that they presented themselves as researchers, operated out of a very nice home, and I found out about them through a bulletin board at Harvard.

A public announcement concerning an experiment appears in a newspaper or such an announcement is received in the mail. The names: 'Stanley Milgram' and the 'Department of Psychology' at 'Yale' are mentioned in the announcement.

Why should anyone feel that she or he should be obedient in relation to any of those names? Stanley Milgram might have been projecting onto his subjects when he supposed that visions of authority and hierarchy would be dancing through the minds of those individuals when they responded to the announcement concerning the 'learning/memory' experiment.

When a subject shows up for the arranged experiment, he or she is not necessarily met by Stanley Milgram. Rather, the subjects are greeted by some 'underling' – who, unknown to the subjects, is actually a biology teacher from an area high school.

Is wearing a white lab coat at Yale University and carrying a clip board enough to induce someone to become obedient? Not necessarily, but it might be enough to induce a given 'subject' to be prepared to cede a certain amount of intellectual and moral agency to such a person who is likely to be perceived as possessing an understanding of the experiment being run and that when that person says 'no serious tissue damage will result from the shocks' being delivered during the experiment, one defers to that sort of a statement because one believes (or hopes) the individual knows what he is talking about ... and not because that person is an authority figure or the representative of a powerful hierarchy.

For example, Professor Milgram attempts to explain the difference in results (48 % versus 65 % of the subjects went to the 450-volt level) between the Bridgeport edition of the 'learning/memory' experiment and the Yale version of the same experiment as being due to the fact that one would expect that subjects would be less likely to be willing to be obedient to, or compliant with, a company – namely, Research Associates of Bridgeport – than they would be willing to be obedient to Yale University, a powerful institution. Alternatively, one also could explain the differences in experimental results between the two editions of the 'learning/memory' experiment by supposing that subjects might consider the members of Research Associates of Bridgeport to be less competent or knowledgeable (or less trustworthy) than researchers at Yale and, therefore, those subjects might be less willing to cede their intellectual and moral agency to the Bridgeport group than the Yale group, and, therefore, more willing to discontinue the experiment in the former case rather than in the latter instance.

Research Associates of Bridgeport – a complete unknown to subjects – might be considered to be willing to let people be injured during the course of an experiment ... after all there are all too many businesses that will hurt people for the sake of profit. On the other hand, Yale University – a much better known entity – might be seen as an organization that would not be willing to let those sorts of things occur ... or, so, the thinking might go.

None of the foregoing considerations necessarily has anything to do with issues of authority, hierarchy, or obedience. The foregoing issues have more to do with what is known or believed or trusted and, whether, or not, one believes that one can cede one's intellectual or moral agency to someone without that ceding process being betrayed.

Throughout the Milgram 'learning/experiment,' subjects are assured that no harm will come to the 'learners.' Yes, the 'learners' might experience some painful shocks, but the subjects are always led to believe – whether implicitly or explicitly – that the 'learners' will be okay.

The issue is not 'obedience' but 'trust'. People are more likely to be willing to cede their intellectual and moral agency when, in some manner, they trust the individual to whom that agency is being ceded.

The researchers at Yale were trusted because they were perceived to have competency with respect to the 'learning/memory' experiment, and this included such matters as whether, or not, anyone might be seriously harmed through that kind of an experiment. However, the point at which someone will retrieve the ceded intellectual and moral agency will vary from person to person.

Some people in the 'learning/memory' experiment were not prepared to let the experiment run very far before they decided that they – rather than the researchers at Yale University – should be the agents who decided how much pain was enough irrespective of what the experiment required. Other individuals were prepared to cede their moral and intellectual agency for a longer period of time ... and some of these individuals were ready to continue ceding

their moral and intellectual agency until the
experiment was called off by the experimenters.

When subjects began to question whether, or
not, it was wise to continue to cede their moral and
intellectual agency to the researchers as a result of
the feedback the 'teachers' were receiving from the
'learners' concerning the pain that was caused
when the toggle switches were depressed, the
person conducting the experiment was always
present to reassure the subject in a calm, non-
threatening manner, that the subjects needed to
continue on with the experiment and, thereby, the
experimenter sent the implicit message that
everything was okay despite the reports of pain
and protest from the 'learner.' Furthermore, when
the 'teachers' mentioned the fact that the 'learners'
were indicating that they did not want to
participate in the experiment any longer, the
person running the experiment indicated that the
'learner's' wishes were irrelevant to the process,
thereby, once again, sending a message to the
'teacher' that despite the pain and protests, it was
okay to continue on with things since, implicitly,
the experimenter was communicating the message
that no one would be, hurt in any serious fashion,
despite the cries and protests of the 'learner'.

The struggle that 'subjects' went through in the
Milgram 'learning/memory' experiment was not
one of whether, or not, to remain obedient to an
authority figure or to the representative of a
powerful hierarchy. The struggle was about

whether, or not, to continue ceding one's moral and intellectual agency to someone who might not necessarily know what they were doing or to someone who might not be trustworthy with respect to protecting everyone's interests.

The more that 'learners' howled with pain and protested the situation, the more 'teachers' were reminded of the nature of the problem with which the latter individuals were faced. Should they continue to cede their moral and intellectual authority to an individual who seemed indifferent to the pain being experienced by the 'learner?'

Did it make sense to continue to trust that kind of an individual – i.e., the experimenter -- to be the keeper of the 'teacher's' moral and intellectual agency? If, and when, an individual broke from the experiment and refused to continue on with the shocks, that person had reached the point where she or he had made the decision to reclaim the moral and intellectual agency that had been ceded to the experimenter at the beginning of the experiment.

Many of the subjects never reached that point. There might have been many reasons for their failure to reclaim their intellectual and moral agency.

For instance, a subject might be experiencing difficulties with: 'self-image;' or, not wanting to have to deal with the possible embarrassment that might be experienced because one chose to opt out of the experiment; or, not wanting to disappoint another individual; or, lack of assertiveness; or, the possibility that by opting out, one might be interfering with the acquisition of knowledge; or, the belief that one should finish a job for which one was being paid; or, not wanting to waste the time of the experimenter by failing to complete the experiment; or, not wanting to have to deal with the possible unpleasantness that might ensue from the conflict or hard feelings that might arise from not continuing on with the experiment. None of the foregoing factors necessarily has anything to do with issues of 'obedience,' 'authority,' or 'hierarchy.'

When the biology teacher who played the 'role' of the experimenter witnessed the distress he was causing the 'teachers' by continually prompting the latter individuals to continue on in the experiment despite their obvious anguish and uncertainty with respect to causing the 'learners' pain, did that biology teacher continue on with what he was doing out of a sense of obedience to Stanley Milgram and Yale University? Surely, the whole experimental set-up would have been explained to him prior to the running of the experiment, and irrespective of whether, or not, the high school biology teacher was being paid for his participation or he was volunteering his services, he probably did not accept the job out of a sense of obedience to either Milgram or the university but did so for other reasons ... reasons (such as curiosity, friendship, wanting a challenge, and so on) to which he conceded his intellectual and moral authority.

Even more to the point, Stanley Milgram did not continue on with witnessing the pain of the 'teachers' as they struggled with their moral and intellectual dilemma out of a sense of obedience to Yale University. He was pursuing his own research interests quite apart from issues of authority and hierarchy relative to Yale University.

Professor Milgram continued to shock his subjects in experiment after experiment after experiment via the moral and intellectual struggle to which he subjected them in the 'learning/memory' research project. He did so because he had conceded his intellectual and moral agency to pursuing a certain kind of research project, and this was done quite apart from issues of obedience, authority, or hierarchy.

A short while ago, I watched a BBC documentary delving into various facets of psychological phenomena. An individual appearing in the program was one of the last surviving subjects of the Milgram 'learning/memory' experiment.

Although the person being interviewed did not appear in Milgram's half-hour video on the experiment, he was one of the many individuals who went all the way to the end with respect to flipping the full set of switches on the electric shock consol. In other words, he flipped switches that, as far as he knew, were apparently inflicting pain on another human being (of which the subject was made aware by the 'cries' of discomfort and protest of the 'learner') and by flipping switches that were clearly marked as being dangerous to deliver to another human being.

Throughout the short interview, it seemed fairly obvious that the former 'subject' in Milgram's experiment still felt regret and, perhaps, even a sense of shame for what he had done nearly half a century before at Yale University. When asked by the BBC interviewer why he had done what he did (that is, flipped all 30 switches on the console), he said: "I lost my moral compass."

He didn't respond in terms of duty, authority, obedience, or compliance. His response appears to indicate that he had ceded his moral and intellectual agency to the experimenters, and, in the process, he had lost his moral way.

What implications, if any, follow from the Milgram 'learning/memory' experiment with respect to the present book? I believe the implications are many and quite direct.

Like the Milgram experiment, the American people have been deceived about and manipulated with respect to the nature of the allegedly democratic experiment that was given expression through the Philadelphia Constitution ... and evidence supporting such a contention has been presented in the first seven chapters of *The*

Unfinished Revolution: The Battle for America's Soul from which the present chapter has been taken. More specifically, the American people have been told that the constitutional process is an exercise in self-governance when nothing could be further from the truth since the ones conducting the experiment have near total control over what transpires within the framework of that experiment.

The reality of the situation is that the Philadelphia Constitution and its concomitant ratification process were an exercise in inducing the subjects in the democratic experiment (i.e., the people) to cede their moral and intellectual authority to the experimenters – that is, the individuals who are conducting the experiment (i.e., the government authorities). Once ceded, the experimenters make use of an elaborate console apparatus that has been constructed by the experimenters (the process of governance) to allow the people to deliver shocks to one another by flipping this or that switch of governance and constitutionally permitted legal maneuvering.

Like Milgram, the individuals conducting the American experiment in democracy, have – after the fact -- put forth the idea that the whole set up of governance is a function of the obedience and sense of obligation that people should feel in the presence of what has been described as "legitimate" authority and hierarchy. Moreover, like Milgram, the ones conducting the experiment in democracy, debrief the citizens in a way that is intended to persuade the latter individuals that being willing to depress toggle switches that those individuals believe will harm other people is quite 'normal' and that it is perfectly 'normal' for the ones conducting the experiment to permit this to happen and that it is perfectly 'normal' for the organizational framework within which this all transpires (Yale University in the case of Milgram and the Philadelphia Constitution in the case of the ones conducting the experiment in democracy) to permit that kind of pathology to continue.

Although the subjects in the Milgram experiment never actually administered any shocks – except to themselves – Milgram, himself administered all manner of emotional and psychological shocks to the individuals he had manipulated to participate in his experiment. Undoubtedly, Professor Milgram believed that the purposes for which the experiment was being conducted were noble ones … even if he didn't actually understand what was going on while he was running his experiments.

Similarly, the individuals – e.g., Madison, Washington, Hamilton, and 53 other individuals who concocted the Philadelphia Constitution – believed that their purposes were noble ones – even if they – like Milgram -- didn't necessarily understand what they were doing. Furthermore, like Milgram, the Founders/Framers were the ones who established a framework that would deliver shocks of various levels of severity to individuals (e.g., Blacks, women, Indians, the poor, the disenfranchised) and, like Professor Milgram, those Founders/Framers (along with their subsequent apologists) sought to rationalize such a set up by pointing to the noble intentions with which their project was supposedly undertaken.

Like the administrators at Yale University in the 1960s, the members of the Continental Congress, looked the other way and permitted something unethical to take place. In other words, just as the members of the Continental Congress permitted the provisions of the Articles of Confederation to be violated by illegitimately transferring the issues surrounding the Philadelphia Constitution over to the ratification process, the Yale University administrators permitted provisions of common, moral decency to be violated through the manner in which the Milgram experiment was allowed to deceive and manipulate people, as well as the manner in which those experiments put their subjects through emotional and psychological turmoil.

The subjects involved in the experiment set in motion through the Philadelphia Convention (i.e., 'We the People') have the same choice that the subjects had in the Milgram experiment. They can continue to cede their moral and intellectual authority to people who do not have their best interests at heart, or those subjects can defy the ones conducting the experiment and opt out of that process.

As is the case in the Milgram experiment, whenever subjects (i.e., citizens) exhibit doubts about the pain that is being inflicted on people via the experiment in democracy, those subjects are 'handled' through the presence of a representative of the experiment (in the form of: government officials, the educational system, the media, and/or the court system). Whenever subjects begin to harbor doubts and are considering the possibility of retrieving the moral and intellectual agency that they ceded at the beginning of the experiment, such handlers, like the biology teacher in the Milgram experiment, say: (1) 'Please continue on;' or, (2) 'The experiment requires that you continue;' or, (3) It is absolutely essential, that you continue;' or, (4) 'You have no other choice, you must go on;' or, (5) 'Although the shocks might be painful, there is no permanent tissue damage, so please go on;' or (6) 'Whether the learner likes it or not, you must go on until he has learned all the word pairs [of democracy] correctly.'

Like the biology teacher in the Milgram experiment, such 'handlers' of democracy use the foregoing prompts – as well as other similar ones -- in a calculated sequence of increasingly rationalized responses that are designed to prevent subjects from retrieving the moral and intellectual agency that such subjects ceded at the beginning of the experiment. The foregoing 'handlers' of democracy are like the sirens of *The Odyssey*, singing seductive songs of vested interests, responsibility, and duty in order to lure unsuspecting sailors (subjects, citizens) to serve the agenda of the ones who are conducting the experiment.

There are, of course, some differences between the Milgram experiment and the experiment in democracy being run through the console of the Philadelphia Constitution. In the Milgram experiment, nothing more than words were used to attempt to induce subjects to continue ceding their moral and intellectual agency to the experimenters. Once subjects understood that the only thing preventing them from retrieving the moral and intellectual agency they had ceded to the experimenters were nothing other than the beliefs and trust of the subjects, themselves, then the subjects were free to disengage themselves from the experiment ... although nearly two-thirds of those individuals were never able to reach this point of realization.

However, in the case of the experiment in democracy that was designed by the Founders/Framers (and continued on by their ideological heirs), realizing that one can retrieve one's moral and intellectual agency (as I did when I was on the bus going to Charlestown Naval Base for purposes of taking a physical to determine my readiness to serve the military during the Vietnam War), is not the end of the story. There are very real extra-linguistic consequences that will be inflicted on any of the subjects participating in the experiment in democracy who have an epiphany concerning the issue of ceding or not ceding one's moral and intellectual agency to the experimenters – that is, the ones who are conducting the experiment in democracy.

Economic sanctions, career sanctions, being socially ostracized, legal sanctions, police action, military intervention, and, of course, being demonized through the media all await anyone who seeks to defy the 'credibility' of the individuals conducting the experiment in democracy by trying to reclaim their moral and intellectual agency. Oftentimes – but not always -- verbal warnings of one kind or another will be given first, and then, when deemed to be necessary, sanctions of one sort or another will be applied in order to discourage the subjects in the experiment from reclaiming their moral and intellectual agency.

Another difference between the Milgram project and the experiment in democracy that was unleashed upon society through the Philadelphia Constitution concerns the size of the 'reward' that is associated with the respective experiments. $4.50 per hour in the Milgram experiment pales in comparison to the thousands and millions of dollars that will be given to individuals who are willing to continue to cede their moral and intellectual authority to the people who are conducting the experiment.

In the Milgram experiment, only words were used to prevent people from reclaiming their moral and intellectual agency. Under those circumstances, nearly two-thirds of the subjects were willing to continue to cede their agency to the experimenters.

When money and other 'perks' enter the picture and are used to subsidize the experiment in democracy, many more than two-thirds of the subjects are likely to be willing to forgo their own moral and intellectual agency in order to continue benefitting, financially and materially, from the experimental set-up. When the punishments that can be brought to bear on individuals who seek to reclaim their moral and intellectual agency are factored in, one should not be surprised that very few of the subjects in the experiment in democracy ever arrive at the point of either wanting to opt out of such a project or to actively follow through on that kind of a desire.

One might venture to hypothesize that one of the reasons why nearly two-thirds of the subjects in certain versions of the Milgram experiment were willing to continue ceding their moral and intellectual authority to the individuals conducting the experiment is because in many societies – including America – people are conditioned from a very early age to cede their moral and intellectual agency to others -- whether these others are: parents, family, peers, teachers, religious figures, politicians, leaders, the military, or the media – who we are told are 'trustworthy.' The presence of a sense of duty in those cases is a function of the conditioning process that is used to induce people to continue on ceding their moral and intellectual agency to those who wish, for whatever reason, to control things by manipulating our sense of – possibly -- misplaced trust concerning them.

In August of 1971, Philip Zimbardo conducted an experiment known as the Stanford Prison Experiment. Apparently, Zimbardo didn't have any deeper insight into his 'prison' experiment than Milgram had with respect to his own 'learning/memory' experiment, and the reason I suspect that the foregoing claim is true is because Professor Zimbardo had to stop his experiment less than six days into a scheduled two week experiment due to serious, unforeseen consequences, and Milgram didn't come up with a theory that purported to explain his experiment (incorrectly I believe) until well after the experiment had ended.

As pointed out previously, the Milgram study is, I believe, an exploration into the realm of ceding and reclaiming moral and intellectual agency in relation to individuals who are (rightly or wrongly) trusted -- and, therefore, it is not (as Professor Milgram claimed) a study concerning the issue of 'obedience.' On the other hand, I believe that the Zimbardo experiment explores (although Professor Zimbardo does not understand his experiment in this way) what happens when people are ceded

authority and, then, proceed to try to leverage what
has been ceded to them in order to control other
people.

Certain subjects in the Stanford experiment –
namely, those who were referred to as 'guards' –
were ceded moral and intellectual agency by
Professor Zimbardo. What I mean by the foregoing
statement is that although Professor Zimbardo was
conducting the experiment, his experimental
design required him to cede some of his own moral
and intellectual authority to those who were
playing the role of 'guards' so that the
experimenters would be able to observe how, or if,
such ceded agency would be used by the 'guards.'

For six days, Professor Zimbardo didn't
understand the nature of the forces that he had set
loose in his experiment. Finally, it dawned on him –
and someone else had to bring him to such a
realization – that he had to stop the experiment
because what was taking place in the experiment
was abusive.

Just as Professor Milgram was an active
perpetrator of abuse in his 'learning/memory'
experiment – although the 'dirty work' was carried
out by the biology teacher who was the face of the
experiment – so too, Professor Zimbardo was an
active perpetrator of abuse in his experiment –
even though the 'guards' in his experiment were
the ones who were doing the actual 'dirty work.' I
believe the foregoing contention is justified
because Professor Zimbardo was the individual

who had enabled some of the guards to do the abusive things they did since, as the individual who was responsible for starting and stopping the experiment, he was the one who ceded to the experimental subjects some of his own moral and intellectual agency in order to permit it to occur.

While Professor Zimbardo would not have understood what he was doing in the following terms, nonetheless, in effect, when he stopped the experiment, he was reclaiming his moral and intellectual agency. Professor Zimbardo, of course, did not see his actions – either at the start of the prison project or in relation to the termination of that experiment -- through the lens of ceding and reclaiming moral agency since he had a quite different theory that will be discussed and critiqued a little later on in the current chapter … but, first, let's take a look at the structural character of the Stanford Prison Experiment.

Like the Milgram experiment, the Stanford Prison Experiment begins with the placing of an advertisement in a number of newspapers. The ads are directed at college students (this is a different target subject pool than was the case in the Milgram 'learning/memory' experiment that wanted to study the actions of people from the general public), and the Zimbardo ad indicates that the proposed study involves some sort of prison experiment.

Those who choose to participate in the experiment will be paid $15.00 a day. Given that the subjects in the Milgram experiment were paid $4.50 for an hour of their time and given that nearly ten years have passed since that experiment had drawn to a close, obviously the value of a student's time is not considered to be worth much … except to those (i.e., the experimenters) who hoped to leverage the situation to gain empirical data that might be of value to them.

The experimental budget totaled just over $5,000 dollars. The money was provided by the Office of Naval Research.

The 14-day experiment is to take place in the basement of the Department of Psychology as Stanford University. A prison-like structure had been built in that location.

Approximately a hundred men respond to the newspaper ads. The potential candidates are interviewed extensively, and they also are administered a variety of psychological tests.

Based on the results of the foregoing interviews and tests, the larger pool of individuals is, then, whittled down to 24 individuals – the experimental sample group. The experimenters have attempted to eliminate anyone who they thought might skew the experiment … such as individuals who have medical or psychological problems, or people with a prior record of arrest.

As far as possible, the experimenters were trying to select average, normal, and healthy individuals. The experimenters were looking for subjects who, in a variety of ways, are fairly representative of middle-class students in general.

Not all of the subjects are full-time students at Stanford. Most of the subjects came from elsewhere in North America and were attending summer school in the Bay area.

The individuals who are finally selected for the experiment are divided into two groups – 'prisoners' and 'guards.' Assigning people to one or the other group is done by flipping a coin ... heads and a student becomes a 'guard', while tails lands a student in the 'prisoner' group.

The 'guards' are not provided with any training. However, those assigned to that group do go through a relatively brief orientation process.

During the latter process, the 'guards' are told that while violence of any kind against the 'prisoners' will not be permitted, nonetheless, the 'guards' are tasked with maintaining law and order, and this includes not permitting any of the prisoners to escape.

There is one further point made to the 'guards' in the orientation process. The experimenters want the 'guards' to create a sense of powerless in the 'prisoners.'

According to Professor Zimbardo, the purpose of his project is to try to develop an insight into the sorts of changes that might take place within an individual – whether a 'prisoner' or 'guard' -- during the course of the experiment. However, the alleged 'purpose' of the experiment is just another way of saying that the experimenters are on a fishing expedition for data and have no clear understanding of what actually will transpire during the experiment ... just as had been the case in the Milgram experiment.

Professor Zimbardo claims that he wanted to determine if it was possible, within the space of two weeks, for subjects – whether 'guards' or 'prisoners' – to assume new identities as a result of the circumstances in which they were embedded. The foregoing intention assumes that Professor Zimbardo understands the nature of identity to begin with – which I don't believe he did any more than most researchers do – and, in addition, Professor Zimbardo seems to have failed to consider the possibility that whatever changes in behavior that might be manifested during the two week period, such changes could be more a reflection of how various social and psychological dynamics can induce different dimensions of one and the same identity to manifest themselves rather than constituting changes in actual identity ... moreover, there is also the possibility that choice – that is, personal agency – could determine that dimension of identity is, or is not, manifested under those circumstances.

After signing release forms, the students who are assigned to the 'prisoner' group are told to be ready and available for the study beginning on Sunday, August 14, 1971. They are not informed about the nature of the means through which they would enter the experiment.

The way in which the experiment starts is, more or less, the same for each of the individuals who have been assigned to the 'prisoner' group. A police car arrives at the 'prionser's' places of residence, and uniformed police officers wearing mirrored, aviator glasses bang on the door of the residence.

'Arrests' are made. Handcuffs and blindfolds are applied to the 'prisoners' – the blindfolds are used to disorient the 'prisoners' and prevent them from knowing where they are going.

The 'prisoners' are placed in the back seat of the cruiser. They are, then, transported to the basement of the Department of Psychology at Stanford University.

Once the 'prisoners' are led down a stairway to the 'prison area,' they are ordered to take off all their clothes. After this is done, the prisoners are told to stand with their arms against the wall with their legs spread apart.

A powder of some kind is thrown on the prisoners. They are told that it is a delousing agent.

Some of the 'guards' begin to make remarks about the size – or lack thereof – of the genitals of the 'prisoners.' Attempts by the guards to humiliate, embarrass, ridicule, and disempower the 'prisoners' have begun.

Eventually -- after a lengthy wait while remaining naked -- the 'prisoners' are given hospital-like, tan gowns to wear. Different numbers are printed across the front of the gowns of each of the 'prisoners.'

The 'prisoners' are not permitted to wear underwear. Consequently, whenever they bend over in their hospital-like gowns, their rear ends are exposed to whoever is nearby.

In addition, the 'prisoners' hair is covered with a nylon stocking. This particular part of the 'prisoner's' attire is intended to serve as the equivalent of the shearing of hair that prisoners experience when processed into actual prisons.

The 'prisoners' are given rubber clogs to wear on their feet. Moreover, a chain is placed around one ankle and locked as a constant reminded of the individual's status as a prisoner.

Once the 'prisoners' have been outfitted in the foregoing manner, their blindfolds are removed. Mirrors have been place against the wall opposite to the 'prisoners' so that they can view the transformation in appearance that has taken place.

'Prisoners' are told they must only refer to one another by the 'numbers' that appear on their hospital-like gowns. Furthermore, 'prisoners' are instructed to address the 'guards' as 'Mr. Correctional Officer.'

162

Events occurring in certain portions of the prison area outside the cells can be videotaped. The camera is hidden.

There is a camouflaged viewing area near the video camera. However, what can be seen and taped is restricted to the area in front of, and near, the location of the viewing area and camera.

Due to considerations of expense, the video camera does not run continuously. It will be turned on only in relation to certain occasions – e.g., during: 'prisoner' count-offs, some meal times, anomalous events of various kinds (such as 'prisoner' disturbances), and a few, scheduled family visits.

The cells of the 'prisoners' are bugged with microphones hidden in the indirect lighting assemblies for each cell. Many – but not necessarily all -- of their verbal comments are capable of being recorded in this way, but the hidden video camera is not able to provide a visual record of what takes place in those cells.

The 'prisoners' are presented with a list of 17 rules. In addition to the already mentioned requirements to refer to the 'prisoners' only by number and to address the 'guards' as 'Mr. Correctional Officer,' the 'prisoners' are also instructed to follow such rules as: Remaining silent during meals, rest periods, and at night, once 'lights out' has been announced; being required to participate in all prison activities; refraining from tampering with or damaging any of the private property in the prison area; reporting all violations of the rules to the guards; obeying all orders that are given by the 'guards; and standing whenever the 'prison' warden or superintendent visits a 'prisoner's' cell.

The 'prisoners' are informed that activities such as smoking or receiving mail and visitors are privileges that can be suspended. Moreover, in any one hour period, the prisoners are only allowed one, five minute visit to the bathroom and those visits will be regulated by the 'guards.'

Finally, the 'prisoners' are told that any failure to comply with the 'prison' rules could be followed by some sort of 'punishment.' Whether, or not, that punishment will occur and the nature of the punishment will be up to the 'guards.'

During the course of the experiment, one of the usual forms of punishment is to order 'prisoners' to do x-number of push-ups for their failure to observe one, or another, of the foregoing 17 rules. However, an isolation box (a small closet in the wall opposite the row of small offices that have been converted to cells) also is available to punish 'prisoners' if the usual methods of punishment prove to be ineffective.

The isolation room is completely dark. It is only big enough to permit an occupant to stand, sit, or squat.

At the 'guards' discretion, the 'prisoners' can be ordered to gather together and commanded to voice, one at a time, the number on the front of their hospital-like gown. These 'prisoner' count-offs are done at certain times – such as in the morning and at night – to determine that all 'prisoners' are present and accounted for, but, eventually, the count-offs will develop a punitive character through which the 'guards' demonstrate to the 'prisoners' that the latter are completely powerless while the 'guards' are all-powerful.

'Prisoners' are told prior to the experiment that they are free to leave the 'prison' at any time. However, whether this rule will actually be honored is another matter, for like the Milgram experiment, there are certain procedures designed to induce 'subjects' to continue on with the experiment.

For instance, as previously indicated, one of the instructions given to the 'guards' is to prevent 'prisoners' from escaping. Presumably, escaping could be understood to be an indication that a 'prisoner' does not want to continue on with the experiment, and, yet, the guards have been instructed to stop the 'prisoners' from escaping ... so how free the 'prisoners' are to disengage from the experiment is a somewhat ambiguous issue.

The 'guards' are divided into three groups. Each group takes a different shift.

The 'guards are outfitted with: Uniforms, sunglasses, whistles, handcuffs and nightsticks. The 'guards' are required to keep a log that is supposed to contain a running summary of what takes place during each shift.

There is 'prison' warden and a 'prison' superintendent. The former individual is played by a psychology student working with Professor Zimbardo, while the 'superintendent' is played by Professor Zimbardo himself.

The foregoing two individuals – along with some other individuals -- are intended to serve in a 'prop'-like or supporting-role capacity in the experiment. They are not considered to be subjects in the experiment.

During the first day, the 'prison' warden informs the 'prisoners' that there will be a 'Visiting Night' in the near future. Subject to the discretion of the 'guards,' 'prisoners' will be permitted to invite members of their family or close friend to visit with them in the 'prison.'

The method of invitation will be through the writing of letters. The warden provides the 'prisoners' with pens for this purpose, but indicates that whether, or not, the letters will be sent will be up to the 'guards.'

The structural character of the 'prison' experiment is designed to induce the subjects who are 'prisoners' to cede their sense of agency much more than is the case with respect to the subjects who are 'guards.' Maintaining law and order through non-violent means is about the only requirement that the 'guards' are required to observe, whereas the 'prisoners' have been assigned a prison identity that is shaped by: 17 rules, plus confinement, and a humiliating dress code.

On the one hand, a sense of agency has not only been taken away from the 'prisoners', but the message is communicated that such 'agency' is not relevant to the experiment. On the other hand, the sense of agency of the guards has been enhanced because the 'guards' have been enabled by the experimenters to do whatever the 'guards' like in relation to the 'prisoners' as long as what is done is of a non-violent nature.

Unlike 'prisoners', 'guards' are implicitly informed -- through the structural character of the experiment -- that their sense of agency does matter to the experiment. The 'guards' are the ones who are to act upon the 'prisoners.'

The 'prisoners' are, in effect, told that in order for them to receive their $15.00 dollars a day, they must give up their sense of agency. The model 'prisoner' is one who has no sense of agency at all.

However, the 'guards' are, in effect, told that in order for them to be able to receive their $15.00 dollars a day, they can do whatever they like as long as they: Do not transgress the guidelines on violence, take their shifts, and help keep a log book. The model 'guard' is one who will 'run' with the sense of 'enhanced agency' that they have been given by the experimenters ... after all, the 'guards' have been provided with no sort of 'moral' or intellectual training to suggest that they should do otherwise.

The 'guards' are implicitly, if not explicitly, informed by the experimenters that their task is not necessarily to be moral 'guards' or 'decent people.' Instead, the 'guards' have been told that a central part of their job will be to make the 'prisoners' feel as powerless as possible and that such a sense of 'powerlessness' is the 'proper' mind-set for a prisoner.

The character of the experiment is heavily skewed toward reinforcing the sense of personal agency of the 'guards', while discouraging the sense of agency among the 'prisoners.' This is not about role playing within a defined social situational context or a matter of how the behavior of individuals will be a function of the situation or the role being played, but, rather, it is a matter of what happens to people when their sense of personal agency is manipulated.

If a person is successfully induced to cede his or her intellectual and moral authority – as is the case with respect to the 'prisoners' in the Stanford Prison Experiment -- then the agency of that sort of an individual will be impaired and, as a result, become dysfunctional. Under those circumstances, an individual is likely to become vulnerable to the whims of those who have retained agency in some fashion within that social framework.

If, on the other hand, a person is successfully induced to believe that his or her agency has been enhanced through the support of a system – for example, the people conducting the prison experiment – and that the only restriction on such an enhanced sense of agency involves avoiding violence, then this sort of individual has been freed or enabled to invest the situation with whatever aspects of his or her imagination or fantasy life that she or he likes ... as long as those investments are deemed to be consonant with the issue of non-violence. Therefore, the 'role' of the guard is ill-defined and open to the interpretation of the individual who is playing the role, while the 'role' of the 'prisoner' is defined in considerable detail and very little room, if any, is left to the interpretive discretion of the individual.

Consequently, the situation or social roles, per se, are not necessarily the determining factor with respect to the behavior of the guards. Rather, what shapes behavior is, in part, a function of what has happened to the realm of personal agency, and whether, or not, that sense of agency has been either undermined in dysfunctional ways or enabled to explore various psychological and emotional possibilities that have not been clearly defined by the experimental situation.

For example, within the first day of the experiment, there is struggle for dominance among some of the 'guards' with respect to how abusive (in a supposedly non-violent way) 'guards' should be toward the 'prisoners.' At least one of the 'guards' already has begun to be quite creative in the ways in which he is prepared to abuse the 'prisoners,' while some of the other 'guards' question whether those sorts of tactics are necessary.

Professor Zimbardo refers to the foregoing process as one of adapting to the role of being a 'guard.' However, since there is nothing in the 'role' of being a 'guard' that says one must seek to dominate other 'guards' or that one must be 'abusive' in creative ways with respect to the prisoner, then this is more a matter of 'guards' inventing that role in the image of their own personalities rather than of 'guards' adapting to some sort of situational role.

Furthermore, when 'guards' are observed to begin taking pleasure in relation to the abuse that they can inflict on other human beings, that pleasure is not a matter of adapting to the role of being a 'guard.' Rather, this dimension of pathology is something that some of the subjects brought with them to the experiment and chose to cede their moral and intellectual agency to during the course of the 'prison' project.

The foregoing facet of things indicates that whatever psychological tests and in-depth interviews have been conducted by Professor Zimbardo, they were not sufficiently sophisticated to provide insight into the pathological potential that can be present in the dynamics of 'normalcy.'

Although the tests and interviews being alluded to above were able to eliminate a variety of people from consideration for the experiment, nonetheless, those same tests and interviews permitted a number of other individuals to slip through the interstitial cracks that were inherent in those evaluation procedures, and these latter individuals were part of the reason why the experiment had to be terminated earlier than scheduled – although, perhaps, the primary reason for the early termination of the experiment might have more to do with the conduct of the experimenters than with the conduct of the 'guards' since the former enabled the latter to transgress certain limits that had been contractually established prior to the experiment being run.

There is also a problem of ambiguity surrounding the meaning of non-violence in the Zimbardo experiment. For example, how does one address the question of: What is the difference between physically assaulting someone and emotionally, verbally, and psychologically assaulting that same individual?

To be sure, physical assault can cause pain, but pain can also be created through verbal and emotional assaults. Physical assaults can leave scars, but this is also true in the case of verbal and emotional assaults. Physical assaults can lead to post traumatic stress disorder, but a great deal of clinical data indicates that verbal and emotional assaults – if sufficiently persistent --can lead to the same sorts of problems.

Abuse is not just about the physical blows that are rained down on an individual. Just as importantly – and, perhaps, more so – is the emotional, psychological and verbal abuse that is directed toward a person.

Perhaps somewhat counter-intuitively, it is the emotional/psychological abuse within, say, a domestic relationship that induces a person to give up their personal agency and remain in a physically abusive environment. Consequently, I find it interesting that the 'guards' in the Stanford Prison Experiment were instructed to do, in a non-violent way, whatever they could to make the 'prisoners' feel completely powerless, and yet, the 'prisoners' were not instructed to do, in a non-violent way, whatever they could to hold onto their sense of personal agency.

There is also a certain amount of inconsistency in the Stanford Prison Experiment with respect to the rule that allegedly prohibits the use of physical violence in relation to the 'prisoners.' During a change of shift in the first day, or so, of the experiment, one of the 'guards' who is leaving the facility yells out to the 'prisoners' and asks them whether, or not, they enjoyed their 'count-offs' during which the 'prisoners' were forced to do all kinds of push-ups and jumping jacks when they didn't count off their 'prisoner' numbers in a way that was pleasing to some of the guards.

One of the 'prisoners' replies from within his cell that he did not enjoy the counts. In addition, the defiant 'prisoner' gives a raised, closed fisted salute and says: "All power to the people!"

Immediately, a number of 'guards:' Storm the cell of the 'lippy' prisoner, physically drag the 'prisoner' to the isolation room (i.e., storage closet), force the 'prisoner' into the closet, and lock the door. How is this not an act of physical violence?

Yet, there is no indication in his book, *The Lucifer Effect*, that Professor Zimbardo intervened in any way and informed the guards that they were not permitted to physically drag 'prisoners' out of their cells or force prisoners into closets. Therefore, while there was a purported rule on the 'books' that said that the 'guards' could not use physical violence, ambiguity was generated – both in the 'guards' as well as the 'prisoners' -- when the rule concerning non-violence was not strictly enforced by the people conducting the experiment.

Another one of the rules imposed on the 'prisoners' concerns the time limit for taking bathroom breaks. The 'prisoners' are only permitted five minutes to finish their business.

Some of the 'prisoners' complain. They claim they are too tense to finish things within the allotted five minute period, but the 'guards' insist on ensuring that the time-limit is observed.

Having experienced the pain of needing to urinate but, for whatever reason, not being able to,

I can empathize with the dilemma of the prisoners. Consequently, intentionally inflicting this kind of pain on someone really is a form of physical violence, and, yet, nothing is said about the situation by the experimenters ... further enabling the 'guards' to physically impose a form of violence on the 'prisoners' despite the presence of the alleged 'no violence' rule.

During an overnight shift, the 'guards' -- in conjunction with the 'prison warden' (who is not an experimental subject ... although, perhaps, he should have been) – come up with a plan for greeting the 'prisoners' during the change in shift that is to take place at 2:30 a.m.. The 'guards' will stand near to the cells of the 'prisoners' and blow their whistles loudly.

The possibility that physically assaulting the ears of sleeping 'prisoners' at 2:30 in the morning might be considered by some to constitute a form of violence seems to escape the 'guards' and, even more inexplicably, the 'warden'. On the other hand, the experimenters already have looked the other way with respect to several forms of physical violence (e.g., dragging a 'prisoner' out of his cell and forcing him into an isolation closet or forcing 'prisoners' to urinate on command), and, therefore, permitting the 'guards' to push the envelope a little more in this direction is allowed to pass by the wayside without comment.

The rude awakening of loud whistles at 2:30 in the morning is followed by a series of physical punishments in the form of forced push-ups and jumping jacks when the 'prisoners' don't perform the count-offs of their numbers to the satisfaction of one, or more, of the guards. The possibility of being dragged off to the isolation room by the 'guards' silently haunts the horizons of the sleepy consciousness of the 'prisoners,' and, therefore, the push-ups and jumping jacks are performed under the threat of physical violence -- of a kind – for any acts of non-compliance ... another 'degree of freedom' extended to the understanding of the 'guards' with respect to the rule concerning no physical violence.

At another point during the first couple of days of the experiment, one of the 'guards' is startled by something that one of the 'prisoners' does and, as a result, pushes the 'prisoner' and, then, uses his fist to hit the 'prisoner' in the chest. Apparently, nothing is said to the 'guard' indicating that such an act is a violation of the 'no physical violence' rule.

On another occasion, a 'prisoner' narrowly misses having his hands – which are extended between the bars of the cell – struck by a nightstick wielded by one of the 'guards' who dislikes how and where the hands of the 'prisoner' have been placed. This is another show of physical violence that is ignored by the people running the experiment.

Again, within a day, or so, of the experiment's beginning, one of the 'guards' takes a cylinder of extremely cold carbon dioxide and sprays it into the cell of several prisoners in an attempt to force the latter individuals to move toward the back of their cell. This would seem to be an act of physical violence – and a potentially dangerous one -- but, apparently, the people running the experiment have labeled it as being something other than what it appears to be.

During another incident, three 'prisoners' are stripped naked and their beds are taken away. I am having difficulty envisioning how forcibly stripping three 'prisoners' naked would not involve acts of physical violence.

Another 'prisoner' has been complaining of a headache. According to Professor Zimbardo's own account of the situation, the 'prisoner' appears to be losing contact with reality and, as well, is expressing a desire to get out of the experiment.

The desire to withdraw from the experiment is ignored. Instead, when the 'prisoner' suddenly jumps up from the dinner table, runs, and, then, rips down the screen that is covering the video camera, he is dragged to the isolation closet, and once inside, the 'guards' continue to bang on the door of the closet with their nightsticks despite the prisoner claiming that the sounds are making his headache worse.

The foregoing incident fully displays the abusiveness and betrayal that permeates the experiment. Despite the fact that the 'prisoner' seems to be losing touch with reality, is behaving strangely, complaining of a headache, and expressing a desire to withdraw from the program, the guards are – without interruption by the people conducting the experiment -- permitted to manhandle the prisoner and commit physical violence against him (and his headache) by pounding their nightsticks on the door of the isolation closet.

To justify their behavior in the foregoing case, the guards go to the rule book that allegedly governs the behavior of the 'subjects' in the experiment. They point to the section involving the rule against 'prisoners' destroying private property in the prison area. However, they seem to be oblivious to the section of the rule book that prohibits the use of physical violence by the guards ... and, in part, they do this because the people running the experiment have enabled the 'guards' to violate those rules with impunity.

During another incident, one of the 'prisoners' refuses to do push-ups. A guard forces the 'prisoner' to go to the ground and, then, presses on the back of the 'prisoner' with a nightstick, telling the 'prisoner to do his push-up.

How is this not an act of physical violence in several ways? Yet, the people conducting the experiment let it go.

The individuals conducting the experiment might wish to object to the foregoing characterizations -- which depicts 'guards' as being permitted to use some forms of 'physical violence' despite the presence of the supposed rule about no physical violence. However, such objections – if they were voiced –tend to resonate with the arguments of those who have attempted to claim that the abuses at: Guantánamo, Abu Ghraib, Bagram Air Force Base, and any number of secret CIA facilities, do not constitute torture because the ones perpetrating the abuses don't agree with how other people define the idea of 'torture'.

In his book, *The Lucifer Effect*, Philip Zimbardo claimed that he made it abundantly clear to everyone that no physical punishment would be permitted during the experiment. Nevertheless, at almost every turn of his project there were forms of physical abuse and punishment that were taking place ... and the examples given here are but a small sample of the sorts of acts of violence that were permitted by the individuals conducting the experiment despite Professor Zimbardo's proclaimed policy of no physical violence or punishments ... apparently one, or more, individuals was in deep denial about the nature of what was transpiring in the experiment.

To be sure, being dragged out of a cell, or being required to urinate within a five minute period, or being forced into an isolation closet, or being forced to do push-ups and jumping jacks, or having loud whistles blown close to one while one is asleep, or nearly having one's hand's crushed by a nightstick, or being sprayed with pressurized carbon dioxide, or having nightsticks pounded against an enclosed space where a person, who seems to be detached from reality, has a headache, might pale in comparison with being gang-raped, killed, and the like, but all of the foregoing acts are points on a continuum of physical violence, and, therefore, to try to argue that because certain kinds of violence are not present that no violence is present at all is, I think, an exercise in sophistry.

At the very least, the individuals conducting the experiment left the 'guards' considerably in the dark with respect to the meaning of 'violence.' As a result, the 'guards' were enabled, if not encouraged, by people running the experiment to shade the possible meaning of 'violence' with various forms of creative abuse of their own – as long as those acts are not ruled out of order (and the people conducting the experiment, like the perpetrators of abuse or torture elsewhere – are serving as the judges in their own cause here). Despite a variety of considerations that might tend to indicate otherwise, Professor Zimbardo appears to believe that such acts are not of a physically violent nature.

If anything, the Stanford Prisoner Experiment suggests just how vulnerable and fragile human beings are when it comes to any sort of violence being perpetrated against them. One doesn't have to use extreme measures of physical violence in order to affect people's sense of personal agency.

Professor Zimbardo claimed that one of the research questions that his experiment sought to address was: What, if anything, would 'prisoners' do to reclaim their sense of personal agency?

Unfortunately, the individuals running the experiment did everything they could to structure the character of the experimental situation in a way that was intended to convince the 'prisoners' that they had no right to a sense of personal agency ... that being able to have a sense of personal agency was not part of the experiment as far as the 'prisoners' were concerned... that in order to collect their pay, the only option that the 'prisoners' had was to play the role of a 'prisoner' as defined by the system.

Like the Milgram experiment involving 'learning/memory,' Professor Zimbardo had sought – unknowingly perhaps -- to manipulate subjects into believing that if they 'trusted' the people conducting the experiment, everything would be okay ... there would be no need to reclaim their sense of personal agency. Like the subjects in the Milgram experiment, the 'prisoner' subjects in the Zimbardo experiment have been led to believe that they should just continue to trust the people conducting the experiment and that nothing of an abusive nature would take place.

The subjects in the Milgram experiment were given the impression that they could discontinue any time they liked, and, yet, subtle steps were taken to prevent people from disengaging from the experiment. Similarly, in the prisoner experiment, the 'prisoners' were given the impression that they could withdraw from the experiment any time they liked, and, yet, subtle – and not so subtle -- steps were taken to prevent the 'prisoners' from remembering that they had such freedom ... for instance, even though the 'guards' were specifically instructed no make sure that the 'prisoners' had no sense of 'personal agency; nevertheless, there were no comparable attempts made prior to the actual running of the experiment to instruct the 'prisoners' that their duty was to assert themselves and defy the guards.

In the foregoing respect, the behavior of the 'guards' was shaped in part by the <u>presence</u> of instructions concerning how they were to engage the experiment. However, the behavior of the 'prisoners' was shaped, in part, by the <u>absence</u> of instruction with respect to the issue of personal agency ... instead they were given 17 rules that were intended to induce the 'prisoners' to forget that they could, if they wish, either discontinue the experiment or seek to reclaim their sense of personal agency by defying the 'guards' in a variety of non-violent ways.

Professor Zimbardo expresses surprise in his book that the 'prisoners' never used the threat of leaving the experiment as a bargaining tool in relation to the abusive treatment they were receiving at the hands of the guards. However, the foregoing perspective does not necessarily correctly describe certain aspects of the prisoner experiment (as will be discussed shortly), and, moreover, even in those facets of the experiment when his observation might be applicable, he never seems to ask himself about the reasons why the 'prisoners' appeared to forget that they supposedly had direct access to such a resource.

The 'prisoners' were attempting to be: 'good,' experimental subjects and meet the expectations of the experimenters by attempting to complete the experiment. They were assuming that the people conducting the experiment would not 'hurt' them, and when that trust was betrayed -- and there can be no question that that trust was betrayed in many different ways, not the least of which was for the experimenters to, on the one hand, proclaim a rule of no-violence and, then, on the other hand, to repeatedly allow that rule to be violated by the guards -- it already was too late because the 'prisoners' felt duty-bound to see the experiment through to the end, just as many of the subjects in the Milgram experiment had struggled to see their experiment through to the end -- despite the anguish, anxiety, and uncertainty they were experiencing – because the 'subjects' trusted the experimenters not to put anyone in harm's way and because the subjects felt a sense of obligation to meet the expectations of the experimenters with respect to the completion of the experiment.

As noted previously, Professor Zimbardo claimed that one of the research questions that was to be addressed by the prisoner experiment was whether, or not, the 'prisoners' would try to reclaim their sense of personal agency and, if they did, then how would they attempt to do this? Why wasn't a similar research question directed toward determining whether, or not, any of the 'guards' would attempt to reclaim their sense of personal agency and, if so, how would they attempt to do so?

Professor Zimbardo's interest in the behavior of the guards arose only after the experiment began. Even then, that interest was shaped by his belief that the 'guards' had fallen under the influence of the powerful gravitational pull of the situation rather than being a function of the way in which people cede their personal agency to this or that force/individual and, thereby, allow their behavior to become influenced by the gravitational pull of a given situation.

Things don't just happen. We make choices about whether, or not, to cede our personal agency to situations, forces, and other individuals ... although on many occasions, those decisions are made so quickly and in the midst of so many different sorts of 'pulls' and 'pushes' that the point of actual transition from: having control over personal agency, to: ceding that agency to a situation, set of forces, or group of individuals, is often only a diffuse, chaotic blur in our memory.

The 'guards' were encouraged to believe that they had considerable degrees of freedom with respect to their own sense of personal agency – a sense of agency that was augmented in a manipulative manner by the people conducting the experiment. Yet, given such an allegedly enhanced sense of personal agency, why didn't any of the guards remove themselves from the experiment – as one-third of the subjects in Milgram experiment had done – due to the abuse that was taking place during that experiment?

The fact of the matter is that both the 'guards' and the 'prisoners' were shackled to the same set of restraints, but in slightly different ways. The sense of personal agency of the 'guards' was manipulated by the researchers to induce the 'guards' to believe that it was okay to be abusive to the 'prisoners,' while the sense of personal agency of the 'prisoners' was manipulated by the researchers to induce the 'prisoners' to believe that it was 'normal' for them to be abused and it was 'normal' to be willing to stay within an abusive system.

Perhaps there are a number of questions here. Why do people stay in abusive relationships? Why are some people willing to abuse other human beings when they are enabled to do so? Why do people continue to stay within a framework that is abusive even if they choose not to directly participate in such abuse and, yet, do not do anything to stop that abuse either? ... something that occurred in relation to some of the 'guards', as well as in relation to most of those who helped conduct the experiment.

With respect to the second question above – that is: Why do people stay in an abusive environment if they do not wish to participate in the abuse but are not willing to do anything to curb the abuse? -- one possible, partial answer does suggest itself. For example, consider the following incident.

One of the guards is showing signs of wanting to disengage from the abuses that are being perpetrated by the 'guards.' The body language of the 'guard' involves hanging his head a lot and walking around the 'prison' with drooping shoulders – suggesting that he is feeling considerable shame.

This 'guard' is constantly volunteering to do things outside of the 'prison' ... such as going for food and coffee. Both his body posture and his interest in spending time away from the 'prison' during his shift indicate that he does not want to be a part of what is transpiring there.

Superintendent Zimbardo tells the warden – one of his students – to talk to the 'guard' and remind the 'subject' that he is getting paid to do a job. The 'guard' is told that in order for the experiment to work, the 'guards' must play their role in a certain way ... that is, with toughness.

Taking a 'guard' aside and telling him what his role is supposed to be is not a matter of a subject adapting to a certain role due to the structural character of the social situation or context. An active intervention of experimenter agency had to take place, and during this intervention the subject had to be provided with instructions concerning the nature of his role.

Interestingly, there were no such interventions in relation to the 'prisoners.' No one took them aside and told them that they should attempt to resist the abuses of the guards ... in fact precisely the opposite sort of intervention took place when Superintendent Zimbardo told the 'prisoners' on the grievance committee that met with him that they were responsible for their own troubles.

Consequently, the 'guards' and 'prisoners' were not necessarily individuals who automatically exhibited certain kinds of behavior because they, somehow, mysteriously adapted to a social role or to the structural features of a given social context – i.e., the prison. Instead, the behavior of the 'guards' and 'prisoners' was shaped, in many ways, through the active intervention of the people conducting the experiment – that is, through the process of personal agency that led to various acts of commission and omission by those who were conducting the experiment.

As unexpected as the results of the prisoner experiment might be with respect to the behavior of either the 'guards' or the 'prisoners,' what I find most surprising in that experimental project is the conduct of the researchers. They stood quietly by and allowed abusive behavior to be inflicted upon their subjects ... and one should not forget that individuals who are induced to commit abuses toward other people are also being helped to be abusive toward their own integrity as human beings – a reminder that applies to both the 'guards' and the 'experimenters'.

Following a 'prisoner' revolt – which consisted of barricading their beds against the doors to their cells so that the 'guards' couldn't get into the cells and that the 'guards' crushed within a fairly short period of time and, then, used as a rationalization to become even more abusive toward the 'prisoners – the "prisoners' formed a grievance committee. The grievance committee listed physical abuse among its complaints.

The committee met with Prison Superintendent Zimbardo. Their complaints are dismissed by the Superintendent who claims that the reason for a great deal of the physical hassling by the guards is due to the bad behavior of the 'prisoners' themselves and due to the fact that the 'guards' are new at their line of work.

Apparently, Superintendent Zimbardo has failed to take into consideration that the 'prisoners' are new to their line of work as well. Furthermore, whether knowingly doing so, or not, the Superintendent has lied to the 'prisoners' because if he has been watching the video and/or listening to the audio or viewing the proceedings from the hidden viewing area, he knows that the 'guards' have done many of the things they have done without any real provocation from the 'prisoners' but, instead, have done so because Superintendent Zimbardo has permitted them to do so – even to the point of continuously permitting the guards to push the envelope with respect to violating the 'no violence' rule.

I find it rather disingenuous of Professor Zimbardo when he claims that he is interested in seeing what steps the 'prisoners' will take to try to reclaim their sense of personal agency when he is simultaneously deeply involved in betraying their sense of trust by demonstrating that he personally approves of the manner in which the 'guards' are violating the no violence rule. The Stanford Prisoner Experiment is not a study about whether, or not, people will try to reclaim their sense of personal agency when certain aspects of their freedom are taken away. Instead, it is a study about the dysfunctional character of the psychological condition that results when individuals are betrayed and, then, subjected to continuous abuse. As a result, 'prisoners' are not really given any legitimate opportunity to regain or develop a sense of personal agency.

On another occasion, one of the 'prisoners' complains about feeling sick and wants to talk with the 'prison' warden. During the meeting, the 'prisoner' refers to the "sadistic" behavior of the guards and indicates that if things don't change, he wants out of the experiment.

The 'warden' follows the path blazed by Superintendent Zimbardo. He tells the individual that the 'prisoners' are the authors of their own misfortune.

Once again, despite the existence of a rule concerning physical violence, the various forms of physical violence being perpetrated by the "sadistic" guards are given a pass ... and the term "sadistic" is not an inappropriate descriptor under the circumstances. Moreover, despite being informed at the beginning of the experiment that the subjects are free to withdraw from the experiment at any time, the 'warden' does not ask the individual if he wishes to disengage from the experiment, but, as was the case in the Milgram experiment, steps are taken to keep the subject in the project.

The aforementioned 'prisoner' goes into an obscenity-laced rage. He demands to see the Superintendent.

The 'warden' tells Superintendent Zimbardo that the 'prisoner' seems deeply troubled by what is going on in the experiment and tells how the 'prisoner' apparently wants to discontinue the experiment. However, the 'warden' isn't sure whether the 'prisoner' is really serious about withdrawing from the experiment or is just saying that he wants out as a tactic of some kind.

Superintendent Zimbardo reports in his book that the 'prisoner' who entered his office is "sullen, defiant, angry, and confused." One of the first things the 'prisoner' says is that he can't go on with things.

The young man is told by the Superintendent – just as was the case in relation to the grievance committee meeting – that he is the author of his own misfortune. In addition, a person who had been recently released from San Quentin and who is helping out in a consulting capacity with the experiment and happened to be in the office when the 'prisoner' came in, begins to verbally abuse the prisoner indicating, among other things, that the little, white, punk sissy wouldn't last a day in a real prison.

Superintendent Zimbardo steps back into the discussion and reminds the 'prisoner' that he will not be paid for the experiment if he quits. The Superintendent asks the 'prisoner' if he needs the money, and the 'subject' indicates that he does.

The 'subject' is propositioned by the Superintendent. Why doesn't the 'prisoner' just cooperate from time to time and the Superintendent will see that the 'guards' won't hassle him.

The 'prisoner' is not sure that he wants to do that. The Superintendent responds with a further proposition that suggests that the 'prisoner' should have a good meal, reflect on the matter, and, then, if the 'prisoner' wants to quit, he can.

The foregoing process – consisting of several propositions and 'negotiations' (which are designed to induce 'prisoners' to remain part of the experiment) -- is not what the 'subjects' were told at the beginning of the experiment. They were told that if they wanted to leave they could, but as was the case in the Milgram experiment, words and warnings are used in the prisoner experiment to

prevent 'subjects' from taking back their sense of
personal agency.

In addition, the Superintendent seeks to
manipulate the 'prisoner's' sense of personal
agency in, yet, another way. Professor Zimbardo is
telling the 'prisoner' that the Superintendent has
the power to tell the guards to lay off the 'prisoner,'
and the Superintendent further implies that if the
'prisoner' will stay with the experiment, the subject
won't be hassled if the individual will just co-
operate from time to time.

The foregoing exchange compromises the
integrity of the experiment in several ways. On the
one hand, if the 'prisoner' is under the impression
that the guards won't hassle him if he co-operates a
little, then, the purpose of the experiment will be
tainted because it supposedly was designed to see
what 'prisoners' would do if their sense of personal
agency was taken away by the 'guards.' On the
other hand, if the Superintendent actually were to
take all of the 'guards' aside and tell them to go
easy on the 'prisoner' this will also compromise the
integrity of the experiment.

If the Superintendent has no intention of
letting the 'guards' in on the
proposition/negotiation process that has taken
place in his office, then he is lying to the 'subject.'
However, if the Superintendent does intend to say
something to the 'guards' concerning the matter,
then he has compromised his experiment.

Prior to meeting with Superintendent Zimbardo, the 'prisoner' had told the other 'prisoners' that he was leaving the experiment. When he comes back from the meeting, he tells the other 'prisoners' that the people running the experiment won't let him leave.

Previously, the trust of the 'prisoners' had been betrayed by the manner in which the people running the experiment continually permitted the 'guards' to push the envelope in relation to physical violence despite the existence of a rule that was supposed to make such acts impermissible. Now, the people conducting the experiment have betrayed the trust of the 'prisoners' in another fashion – namely, apparently, despite assurances otherwise, the 'prisoners' were not going to be permitted to leave the experiment ... they really were 'prisoners.'

The people conducting the experiment claim that the essential theme of their project is to discover what people will do when their sense of personal agency is degraded, if not eliminated. Nevertheless, the actual nature of the experiment is about what happens to people when their sense of trust is betrayed and, as a result, they become exposed to abusive treatment as a direct result of that betrayal.

The 'prisoners' answered an ad in which successful candidates would exchange some time for money. Instead, they became entangled in a nightmare ... something for which they had not signed up.

Professor Zimbardo claims that the aforementioned 'prisoner' who said he wanted out of the experiment and came to Zimbardo after seeing the 'warden' should never have agreed to become a 'snitch. Moreover, Professor Zimbardo says that the individual should have insisted on being let out of the experiment but was cowed into backing down when harangued by the person who had recently been released from San Quentin.

I believe the foregoing explanation is not tenable and is rather self-serving. To begin with, the prisoner who complained to Superintendent Zimbardo didn't agree to become a snitch – that is, someone who provides information about other prisoners in exchange for lenient treatment from the 'guards.

Instead, Superintendent Zimbardo was the one who proposed that if the 'prisoner' would stay in the program, co-operate a little, then the Superintendent would arrange to have the guards ease up on their hassling of the 'prisoner.' Therefore, Professor Zimbardo is seeking to re-cast his attempt to save his own experiment as an exercise in mind-games by the prisoner who Professor Zimbardo incorrectly claims made a deal to become a 'snitch.'

Secondly, Professor Zimbardo impugns the character of the 'prisoner' by claiming that the individual was cowed into silence concerning the issue of wanting out of the experiment due to the tongue lashing that the 'prisoner' got from the person who recently had been released from San Quentin and was serving as a consultant for the prisoner experiment. Again, Professor Zimbardo is re-casting events in a manner that is favorable to himself, because the reality of the situation is that the 'subject' wanted to get out of the experiment, and Professor Zimbardo wouldn't let him do so despite the subject having given clear indications that he did not want to participate in the project any further.

Another 'prisoner' becomes depressed, despondent and glassy-eyed. He lies on his cell floor coughing and asks to see the Superintendent.

Apparently, the 'prisoner' also wants out of the experiment. Although the Superintendent tells the 'subject' that he can get out if he wants to, the Superintendent also seeks to induce to 'prisoner' to continue to cede his sense of personal agency, stay in the experiment, and just co-operate with the 'guards.'

Professor Zimbardo has moved the goal posts. At the beginning of the experiment, he told the 'subjects' that they can leave the experiment at any point. Afterwards he takes steps to keep the 'subjects' in the experiment despite their wishes to do otherwise.

Later on, one of the 'prisoners' is finally allowed to withdraw from the experiment. The decision to allow the 'subject' to leave was not

made by Professor Zimbardo but by a 2nd year
graduate student.

According to the foregoing graduate student,
the individuals conducting the experiment were
never quite sure whether, or not, the 'prisoners'
were faking their complaints. Moreover, because a
lot of money and time had been invested in the
experiment, they were reluctant to let anyone leave
the experiment because of the way such actions
might compromise the experimental results.

Why was a second-year graduate student
making those kinds of decisions rather than
Professor Zimbardo? If the people conducting the
experiment couldn't tell the difference between
real trauma and feigned trauma, why were they
involved in the experiment at all? Why didn't
Professor Zimbardo have any clinical psychologists
directly affiliated with his research project? Why
were the people running the experiment more
concerned about the time and money that had been
invested than the physical and mental welfare of
their 'subjects'? And, finally, even if the complaints
of the 'prisoners' were faked, why didn't the
experimenters keep their word and let the
'prisoners' go when some of the latter individuals
indicated that they had enough?

After the prisoner being alluded to above was
released, one of the guards overheard a plot by
some of the remaining 'prisoners' that allegedly
involved the released prisoner coming back with a
bunch of friends in order to free the 'prisoners' and

destroy the 'prison.' Although the people conducting the experiment considered the alleged plot to be a somewhat unlikely possibility, credence was given to the story when the released prisoner was reported by one of the 'guards' to be skulking about in the hallways of the Psychology Department in the floors above the basement area where the 'prison' was housed.

As a result, Superintendent Zimbardo ordered the 'guards' to capture the released 'prisoner' and return that individual to the 'prison.' Superintendent Zimbardo decided that the 'prisoner' had been faking things and was not really in emotional or physical difficulty.

Despite assurances to the participants that they could leave the experiment whenever they wanted to, there now seemed to be an unwritten rider invisibly and secretly inserted into the rules governing the prison. If a 'prisoner' decides he wishes to withdraw from the experiment and is released, but later on the people running the experiment decide the person was only feigning distress, then, the experimenters reserve the right to bring that person back into the project.

Why did Superintendent Zimbardo accept the word of a 'guard' without any corroborating evidence? Was the 'guard' one of those who was abusing the 'prisoners' and, therefore, had a hidden motive to lie about or exaggerate the nature of what he reportedly witnessed? Did the former 'prisoner' have a right to be in the Psychology

Department? Was the former 'prisoner' actually skulking about the halls of the psychology building or was the description of that person's behavior either a prevarication or a biased observation? And, once again, irrespective of the 'feigning' issue, why didn't the individual have a legitimate right to withdraw from the experiment.

The foregoing questions are not irrelevant to what was taking place in the prisoner experiment. Later on, Professor Zimbardo came to the conclusion that the whole plot to storm the prison is nothing but a 'rumor' and that all their elaborate arrangements – such as packing the 'prisoners' into a windowless, poorly ventilated storage room elsewhere in the psychology building for three hours – were completely unnecessary ... and, yet, such actions were taken because one of the subjects (a 'guard') had induced the experimenters to cede their sense of personal agency to the uncorroborated word of a 'guard' who might have ulterior motives for saying what he did.

Professor Zimbardo confesses that the "biggest sin" in behaving in the foregoing way is that they did not systematically collect data with respect to the events of that day. Actually, their biggest sin was, apparently, to be so completely oblivious to not only the 'abusive' system they had set in motion but to be so completely oblivious to their role in nurturing that abuse.

In later years, Professor Zimbardo will interpret the experiment as one in which the 'experimenters' as well as the subjects came under the gravitational influence of the situation. However, what Professor Zimbardo still does not seem to understand is that the process of coming under the gravitational influence of a situation is a function of people – each for different reasons – making a decision to cede their intellectual and moral agency to the forces inherent in that kind of a situation.

A situation by itself is powerless. It requires the co-operation of someone with agency ... that is, someone with the capacity to make choices about whether, or not, to cede agency to some situation, individual, or group.

At one point in *The Lucifer Effect*, Professor Zimbardo indicates that it "seems" that some of the 'guards' have been denying the 'prisoners' access to the bathroom after the order for 'lights out' has been given. One wonders why the term 'seems' is used ... how did Professor Zimbardo acquire the information to which the term "seems' is affixed?

According to Professor Zimbardo, the 'prison' area is beginning to smell like a subway washroom. Somehow, he knows that the 'guards' have been requiring the 'prisoners' to relieve themselves into buckets that are in their cells.

In the same section of his book, Professor Zimbardo discloses knowledge about how some of the 'guards' have been reported to be tripping blind-folded 'prisoners' as the latter individuals make their way down a set of stairs leading to the bathroom. In addition, these same guards apparently enjoy poking the 'prisoners.'

One of Professor Zimbardo's observations concerning the foregoing pieces of information is that some of the 'guards' have transcended mere role playing and, instead, have "internalized the hostility, negative affect, and mind-set" qualities of actual guards in real prisons. Nothing has been internalized.

The individuals displaying the pathological behavior brought that potential with them when they entered the experiment. Neither the allegedly in-depth interviews, nor the psychological tests that were given, were able to detect the presence of those pathological inclinations.

The foregoing sort of pathological inclinations were not the result of role-playing or any mechanism of internalizing the mind-set of actual guards. Those inclinations were nurtured – unknowingly perhaps – by the manner in which the people running the experiment failed, among other things, to enforce the rule requiring 'guards' not to be physically violent toward the 'prisoners.'

Some 'subjects' came to the Stanford Prisoner Experiment with a potential for certain kinds of abusive behavior. The individuals conducting the experiment provided that potential with the opportunity to be expressed within the context of the experiment and, then, the people running things did nothing to curb that behavior once it started to be manifested.

The prison-situation, per se, did not induce such a dispositional potential to surface. What caused that behavior to be expressed was the intervention of the experimenters through their acts of commission and omission with respect to their rule about physical violence and their failure to hold the 'guards' accountable for the latter's repeated transgression of that rule.

Professor Zimbardo indicates that the 'prison' and the 'prisoners' will have to be put in a better light when the parents, friends, and girlfriends of the 'prisoners' visit the prison. In other words, according to Professor Zimbardo, the experiment requires not only for the 'subjects' to be manipulated, but, as well, he believes that the impressions of visitors will have to be managed ... after all, Professor Zimbardo is of the opinion that: "As a parent, I surely would not let my son continue in such a place if I saw such exhaustion and obvious signs of stress after only three days."

The foregoing admission is disturbing on a number of levels. For instance, if as a parent, Professor Zimbardo would not permit his son to continue on in such a set of circumstances, why does Professor Zimbardo suppose it is okay for him to put his subjects in 'harm's way given that he – unlike the forthcoming visitors -- is actually somewhat cognizant of what is taking place in the 'prison'? Secondly, knowing what he knows about the situation, apparently Professor Zimbardo feels it is okay to manipulate the impressions of the visitors so they won't constitute a threat to the continuation of the experiment.

On the day when parents, friends, and girlfriends are supposed to visit the 'prison,' the facilities and the 'prisoners' are washed, disinfected, and spruced up. The smell of urine and feces are covered up with the scent of a deodorizer, and the 'Isolation Room' sign is taken down.

'Prisoners' are told that if they complain to the visitors during the visits, the visits will be terminated prematurely. The instructions resonate with what the Nazis used to do when the Red Cross showed up ... making threats to the prisoners in order to prevent outsiders from coming to know what actually was taking place in a given stalag.

That the people conducting the experiment apparently found it necessary to dupe the relatives and friends of their 'prisoners,' is extremely disconcerting. Manipulating and betraying their subjects is bad enough, but, they also felt compelled to manipulate and betray people outside the experiment, and the reason the deception is considered necessary is because – on some level -- the people running the experiment were aware that something pathological was taking place during the experiment, but, unfortunately, they weren't ready to close down that kind of process.

Professor Zimbardo recounts how the people conducting the experiment came to the conclusion that they had to bring the visitors under situational control. This meant that the experimental staff was tasked with having to induce the visitors to believe that they – i.e., the visitors – were nothing but guests who were being extended a privilege.

The foregoing is an exercise in dissembling. The idea of bringing something under "situational control" is merely a euphemism for lying to people and misleading them, and through such a process, inducing outsiders to cede their sense of personal agency to the experimenters through the manipulation of trust.

The experimenters should not have been trusted by the visitors. Furthermore, in a number of ways, the experimenters were aware that they should not have been trusted, and this is why things had to be brought under so-called "situational control."

Despite the experimenters' best efforts to cover up the pathology taking place within the prison, some of the reality leaked through the attempts of the experimenters to take situational control and mislead the visitors about the nature of what was transpiring in the basement of the psychology building. Following the 'visitor night,' Professor Zimbardo received a note from a mother of one of the 'prisoners.'

She remarked that she had been troubled by the appearance of her son during the visit. She also indicated that prior to the experiment neither she nor her son had contemplated that anything so 'severe' would be involved with respect to the experiment.

Several more days of experimental treatment had to take place before a decision was made by the experimenters to release her son. Apparently, they concluded that the young man was exhibiting signs of acute stress ... a diagnosis that the mother had tried, in her own words, to communicate to the experimenters a few days earlier – too bad the experimenters hadn't hired her as a consultant for she seemed to have more sense than they did.

On the fourth day of the experiment, Professor Zimbardo has arranged for a real priest to come to the 'prison' in order to interview the 'prisoners.' The priest has had experience as a prison chaplain, and Professor Zimbardo wants to get some feedback from the priest with respect to how 'realistic' he feels the experiment is.

The interviews take place in the 'prison.' One at a time, the 'prisoners' come and talk with the priest.

Many of the 'prisoners' introduce themselves by reciting the number on the front of their 'hospital-like' gown. According to Professor Zimbardo, the priest displays no indication that he finds the behavior of the guards in this respect to be odd.

Professor Zimbardo considers the priest's lack of reaction to be surprising. The professor concludes that: "Socialization into the prisoner role is clearly taking effect."

Although the section in which the foregoing quote appears is somewhat ambiguously written, apparently Professor Zimbardo is of the opinion that the priest has been socialized into the role of the prisoners by not reacting to their manner of introducing themselves by number rather than name. In other words, Professor Zimbardo is surprised by the behavior of the priest and seeks to explain it by claiming that the priest has been socialized into the mind-set of the prisoners.

The foregoing account of things is consistent with Professor Zimbardo's belief that people adapt to social situations because their natural dispositions come under the influence of situational forces. Absent from such a perspective is an explanation about how anyone – for example, the priest -- comes under the influence of those forces.

Socialization is not an automatic phenomenon. Interpretations, judgments, and choices are made concerning whether, or not, to cede one's agency to the forces of socialization.

Professor Zimbardo already has ceded his moral and intellectual agency to the prisoner experiment – which is why he is willing to let abusive behavior take place. He would only be surprised by someone else also ceding their sense of agency as well if he is inclined to ignore the nature of the process through which a person's sense of personal agency is ceded to a given situation and, instead, believes that a process of 'socialization' has somehow mysteriously taken effect sooner than anticipated.

The priest played his role to the hilt. He asked the 'prisoners' about bail conditions, whether, or not, they had lawyers or if they would like him to contact anyone on the 'outside' for them.

Professor Zimbardo assumed that the priest's offer to contact people on the 'outside' was merely a façade with respect to the role the priest was playing. When the priest is questioned by Professor Zimbardo about the offer, the experimenter is surprised to discover that the priest considers it a duty to follow through on his offer to the prisoners.

The foregoing incident demonstrates one of the differences between the priest and Professor Zimbardo. The priest has not ceded certain aspects of his moral agency to the experiment, and, therefore, unlike Professor Zimbardo, when the priest promises something, he feels obligated to follow through on the promise.

On the other hand, the priest has ceded some degree of agency to Professor Zimbardo because the priest seems to accept certain things that are going on in the prison but, presumably, believes that Professor Zimbardo is not the sort of person who would place students in harm's way ... in other words, the priest has conceded a certain amount of trust to the professor, but like the visitors the night before, the priest should not have trusted the professor because the experimenter has imprisoned the 'subjects' in a highly abusive situation.

While the priest is interviewing one of the 'prisoners,' the subject complains of a headache and indicates that he feels anxious and exhausted. Following some questions by Professor Zimbardo directed toward the 'prisoner' in order to discover the cause of the headache, the 'prisoner' breaks down in tears.

The priest speaks to the 'prisoner' and indicates that, perhaps, the prisoner is bothered by the unpleasant smell that pervades the 'prison.' He considers the smell rather toxic in nature, but he also believes that it helps lend a sense of realism to the experiment.

The priest doesn't know how that smell came to permeate the atmosphere. If he did, he might not have been so willing to merely comment on the smell and, then, move on to other things.

The priest has been asked to comment on how realistic the 'prison' experiment is relative to the real thing. He hasn't been asked to make an evaluation on whether, or not, the 'prisoners' are being treated properly.

He trusts that they have been treated properly because he believes that Professor Zimbardo is the sort of person who would not permit students or subjects to be treated in an abusive manner. Since the priest is not willing to entertain the possibility that something pathological is taking place, he misdiagnoses the breakdown of the 'prisoner' as possibly being a reaction to the unpleasant smell in the 'prison.'

After interviewing the 'prisoners,' the priest provides his overview of what he has observed. He indicates that the experimental prison seems to be operating much as a real prison does and, as a result, many of the 'prisoners' are exhibiting what he refers to as "first-offender syndrome" – that is, the 'prisoners' are exhibiting signs of: irritability, if not rage, as well as depression and confusion.

The priest indicates that the symptoms are likely to dissipate after a week, or so. He refers to the behavior as being effeminate in nature and comments that inmates in real prisons learn that such conduct is not conducive to long-term survival.

What the priest does not suspect is that what he refers to as "first-offender syndrome" is actually a function of another kind of phenomenon altogether. The priest is looking at the behavior of the 'prisoners' through the lenses of actual prison life – and the priest has been induced to do so due to the manner in which the experimental situation has been presented to him by Professor Zimbardo.

The professor believed he had to take situational control of the visitors the night before because he knew that the parents would never approve of what was taking place in the prisoner experiment if they were to come to know the truth of what was transpiring in the 'prison.' Obviously, if Professor Zimbardo knew that what was going on in the prison was sufficiently problematic for it to be necessary to manipulate the impressions of the visitors, then he is not likely to be willing to confess to the priest concerning the pathological character of what has been happening in the basement of the psychology building ... the impressions of the priest have to be managed just as the impressions of the visitors had to be handled through the process of taking situational control and, thereby, using disinformation and misinformation to shape people's understanding of the situation.

If the priest knew about the actual nature of the betrayal, and ensuing abuse, that was entailed by the prisoner experiment, would he continue to say that the behavior of the 'prisoners' was merely a reflection of the "first-offender syndrome" that takes place in actual prisons, or would he be prepared to state that what was going on in the experiment was abusive and pathological. One would like to hope that the priest would have been willing to change his opinion about what was transpiring in the 'prisoner' experiment, but in the light of what has taken place in the Catholic Church concerning the issue of sexual abuse, one is not entirely sure what the priest might have done.

According to Professor Zimbardo, the priest's visit helped demonstrate the progressive nature of the conflation and confusion that is occurring with respect to the character of the relationship between reality and delusion during the prisoner experiment. He claims that the priest played his role of prison chaplain so well that the performance has helped transform the fiction of an experiment into a reality of its own.

Like the 'prisoners' and the 'guards', Professor Zimbardo had ceded his moral and intellectual agency to the delusional pathology that had taken over the experiment. The priest, on the other hand, was merely fulfilling a request by Professor Zimbardo to assess what was going on in the 'prison' and whether, or not, those conditions reflected actual prison life.

In order to gather the data necessary to make such an assessment, the priest played a role. As soon as the priest walked away from the role, he provided Professor Zimbardo with a comparative analysis of the situation.

The priest might have been operating under a misunderstanding with respect to what actually was going on in the 'prison' experiment, but he had not confused delusion with reality. With the exception of the issue of trusting Professor Zimbardo when, perhaps, the priest should not have done so – although such acts of ceding agency through trusting others often takes place in society every minute and hour of the day -- the priest had not ceded his sense of personal agency to the prison experiment except to the extent of temporarily playing a role that he knew was just a role.

The foregoing cannot be said with respect to Professor Zimbardo. He had ceded away his sense of personal agency to the experiment and, as a result, he permitted events to take place in the experiment that might not have occurred if he had not ceded such agency and, thereby, permitted himself to become entangled in a delusional world.

To be fair, there were times during the experiment when Professor Zimbardo reclaimed some degree of his sense of personal agency and disengaged from the delusional world of the prison experiment. For instance, on one occasion he found a 'prisoner' -- who previously had been exhibiting signs of acute stress – in a condition of hysterical meltdown, and Professor Zimbardo reminded the 'prisoner' that he was a student with a name and not just a number and that the 'prisoner' should withdraw from the experiment and go home. Professor Zimbardo wants to take the individual to see a doctor on campus.

The 'prisoner' stops crying and trembling. He stands up and insists on going back into the experimental prison.

The 'prisoner' says that he does not want to leave under circumstances in which he is being labeled by the other 'prisoners' as a 'bad' prisoner and whose behavior might result in the other 'prisoners' being harassed by the guards. Unlike all too many of the guards, perhaps the 'prisoner' has not ceded his sense of moral decency to the experiment, and, consequently, he wants to do the 'right' thing by the other 'prisoners,' himself, and the experiment.

On the other hand, maybe the desire of the 'prisoner' to remain in the experiment is merely a variation on the 'Stockholm Syndrome.' In other words, perhaps, the allegiances of the 'prisoner' have been captured by the delusional nature of the 'prison' experiment, and, as a result, the 'prisoner' is having difficulty understanding that his desire to do 'right' by the experiment might merely be an expression of how much agency he has ceded to the experiment and why he feels inclined to remain in the experiment when he has the opportunity to escape an abusive situation.

On another occasion, Professor Zimbardo also reclaims a certain modicum of the moral and intellectual agency that he has ceded to the idea of the experiment when he intervenes with the 'guards'. He instructs them that they must not interfere with visiting hours.

Apparently, the 'guards' are upset with this sort of limitation that has been placed upon their conduct by Professor Zimbardo. However, they comply with the directive.

One wonders why Professor Zimbardo didn't take the steps necessary to rein in their power with respect to far more serious instances of abusing the rights of the 'prisoners. Perhaps, he was beginning to become a little more aware of the injurious impact that the abusive treatment of the 'guards' was having on the prisoners.

Professor Zimbardo might have had some assistance with respect to his condition of possibly enhanced awareness concerning the issue of abuse. After a number of 'prisoners' were permitted to withdraw from the experiment, Professor Zimbardo added a new 'prisoner.'

Despite the 'prisoner's' fear of the guards – he had been struck on the leg by a nightstick while being stripped naked and deloused – once initiated into the experiment, the new 'prisoner' went on a hunger strike. The hunger strike was intended to protest the manner in which the 'guards' were violating the conditions of the contract with respect to, among other things, the use of physical violence.

The 'prisoner' indicates that when he signed the contract to participate in the experiment, there were certain provisions in that document concerning the conduct of the guards. The 'guards' were violating those conditions, and the 'prisoner' made sure that everyone heard him with respect to that issue.

At least some of the 'guards' don't seem to care about the part of the contract that concerns their own behavior. They are only interested in the parts of the contract that cover the conduct of the 'prisoners' since violation of those portions of the contract enable the 'guards' to rationalize their abusive treatment of the 'prisoners.'

Such 'guards' have a vested interest in selectively reading the contract for the experiment because, apparently, they have begun to enjoy the abuse that they are inflicting on the 'prisoners.' However, the 'experimenters' also have a vested interest – namely, to keep the experiment going – to look the other way when the 'guards' violate sections of the contract (few though these sections might be) that govern the conduct of the guards.

During most of the first five days of the prison project, the experimenters have enabled some of the 'guards' to believe that the contractual rules that addressed the behavior of the 'guards are not relevant to what goes on in the experiment. Only very occasionally – such as when Professor Zimbardo instructed the guards not to interfere with the visiting hour arrangements – did the experimenters honor the contract that they, themselves, had drawn up, and, quite possibly, the fact that at least one of the experimenters reclaimed some semblance of moral and intellectual agency with respect to the experiment was triggered by individuals like the new 'prisoner' who kept reminding the 'guards' – and, perhaps, Professor Zimbardo -- that their behaviors were violating the terms of the contract.

The experiment begins to crumble toward being shut down when someone with whom Professor Zimbardo is romantically involved begins to insert a few rays of moral agency into the darkness of the 'prison' project. Previously, she had played only a small role in the drama when she served on the Parole and Disciplinary Board, but she had never visited the 'prison' or had any inkling of what actually was taking place there.

On the fifth day of the experiment, she is invited down to the 'prison.' Prior to reaching the 'prison' she has a conversation with one of the 'guards,' and based on that conversation, she comes away with the impression that the individual seems to be a very nice young man.

A short while later she is observing the 'prison' experiment through the hidden portal that is near the video camera. She is appalled that the individual whom just a short while earlier had left her with such a favorable impression is now engaged in mean and abusive behavior.

The transformation in conduct seems incredible. The individual is: talking, walking and acting in a manner that is completely different than had been the case when he was outside the building talking with her.

Professor Zimbardo tries to direct her attention to something that is going on in the 'prison.' She seems uninterested in what he is excited about, and, in response, Professor Zimbardo tries to justify what is going on as constituting a phenomenon involving human behavior that, up until then, was unknown and unsuspected ... other members of the experimental staff who are present take the professor's side in the matter.

Tears are streaming down her face, and she tells Professor Zimbardo that she is going home. He catches up with her outside the building and begins arguing with her and barraging her with belittling remarks concerning her potential for ever being a competent researcher if she can't manage her emotions better than what she is presently doing.

He explains to her that many people have visited the 'prison' and none of them have reacted to the situation in the way she has. He claims that they didn't find anything wrong with what was going on in the prison experiment.

The fact of the matter is that Professor Zimbardo is not being honest when he makes the latter sort of claims. First of all, no one outside of the experimental staff actually witnessed the sort of abusive treatment that was being inflicted on the 'prisoners' by the guards.

The priest who had been permitted into the 'prison' for a short time only interviewed the 'prisoners.' He did not observe any of the 'normal' interaction between the 'guards' and the 'prisoners' ... although the priest did smell one dimension of that interaction.

Moreover, the relatives and friends who had attended the 'Visitors Night' did not witness any of the pathological behavior that was taking place in the prison. However, one of the mothers wrote a note to Professor Zimbardo indicating – based on the appearance her son – that she was concerned about her son's mental and physical health.

By his own admission, Professor Zimbardo had to take situational control of such situations. Otherwise, people might become aware of the abuses that were taking place in the basement of the psychology building and, therefore, he believed he had to manage people's perceptions about what was actually happening in the experiment ... a tacit acknowledgement that the experiment was not as 'innocent' as he was attempting to convince people – including himself -- was the case.

For five days, Professor Zimbardo carried around within him knowledge – at least on some level – that what was taking place in the 'prison' was pathological and abusive. It took only a very short time for the woman with whom he was romantically involved to recognize and understand some of the unseemly underbelly of what he had been up to in his experiment.

The two had further arguments about the matter. She told Professor Zimbardo on several occasions that the young men in the experiment were suffering and that terrible things were being inflicted on those "boys."

She was extremely concerned because like the guard with whom she had talked prior to venturing down into the 'prison,' she had viewed Professor Zimbardo as someone who was caring, kind, and compassionate. Yet, Professor Zimbardo was supervising an experiment in which there seemed to be little evidence that could demonstrate the presence of such a caring, kind, or compassionate person, and, like the guard, the individual (i.e., Professor Zimbardo) that she thought she knew was actually acting in a way that was contrary to what she had expected.

Following their discussion, the professor decides to end the experiment. When Professor Zimbardo returns to the 'prison,' he discovers that the 'guards' have invented a new form of abuse in which the 'prisoners' are required to mimic sex acts with holes in the floor and with one another whenever the 'prisoners' displease the 'guards.'

Professor Zimbardo concludes that most of the 'guards' were unable to resist the situational temptations of control and power. On the other side of the ledger, Professor Zimbardo feels that most of the 'prisoners' had suffered varying degrees of physical, mental and emotional breakdown under the situational forces that impacted on them.

Unfortunately, Professor Zimbardo does not seem to understand that what has gone on for five days has little to do with people being transformed by situational temptations and forces. Instead, the experimenters enabled the entire pathology of the 'prison' experiment to occur as a result of their failure to enforce the contractual 'right' of the 'prisoners' to be free from physical violence as well as their failure to hold the 'guards' accountable for their many transgressions against that 'right'.

The experimenters were caught up in the delusion that they were objective researchers who were pursuing noble, ground-breaking ends. Consequently, they were more interested in keeping the experiment going than they were concerned about the welfare of their subjects – whether 'guards' or 'prisoners' -- and, as a result, they continued to permit the areas of 'problematic conduct' in relation to the 'guards' to be broadened ... for to have done otherwise would have prevented the 'guards' from doing what they did, and what they did were the sorts of behavior that not only seemed to intrigue the experimenters but that had such 'interesting' effects upon the 'prisoners.'

One of the questions hovering about the Milgram and Zimbardo experiments is the following one. Why did both experiments, each in its own way, permit abuse to be perpetrated in relation to subjects?

If either of the foregoing researchers had, to a sufficient degree, critically reflected on their respective experiments prior to the fact of those experiments being run, they might have considered the possibility that there were abusive dimensions to their research projects. In other words, whatever the 'teachers' might have 'done' (or believed they were doing) to the 'learners' in the Milgram experiment, and whatever, the 'guards' might have done to the 'prisoners', both Professor Milgram and Professor Zimbardo should have understood that the experimental process to which they were going to expose their subjects was inherently abusive ... if for no other reason than that the <u>trust</u> which subjects placed in the people conducting the experiment (and if trust had not been present, the subjects are not likely to have been inclined to participate in such a process) would be betrayed when, in one way or another, the subjects' sense of personal agency was manipulated, and then, the two experiments – each in its own way -- proceeded to hold that sense of agency hostage to the agenda and purposes of the various researchers.

Neither Professor Zimbardo nor Professor Milgram had a right to the sort of intellectual freedom that entitles them to abuse other human beings for the purposes of discovering something that might be of interest or even of value. The law of ignorance says that the boundaries of one's right to push back the horizons of ignorance extends only to being provided with a fair opportunity to do so, and this sort of fairness entails a reciprocal obligation not to undermine anyone else's right to have the same kind of fair opportunity to be able to proceed in a similar fashion.

When people are deceived and manipulated, the quality of fairness is significantly degraded if not entirely eliminated. What the alleged purpose of such deception and manipulation are is irrelevant to the issue of fairness and its inherent quality of reciprocity.

Just as the Milgram learning/memory experiment carried many implications for issues of governance, there also are many parallels between the Stanford Prison Experiment and the issue of governance. While there were many mistakes made in the Zimbardo experiment that are important to grasp because that sort of understanding might serve to guide one in relation to how <u>not</u> to conduct research, the prisoner experiment might be more important as an illustration of the pathological dynamics that often occur within almost any framework of governance.

For example, the Philadelphia Constitution is often portrayed as an experiment in democracy. However, like the Stanford Prisoner Experiment, the people who dreamed up the idea for such an experiment didn't necessarily know what they were doing or how things would turn out.

During the Constitutional ratification process, when people asked questions about how the Philadelphia document would work, the supporters of ratification had worked out stock, theoretical answers and these were fed back to the people asking the questions. Those answers were entirely theoretical and speculative because no one had previously tried such an experiment, and, consequently, there was little hard data to support any of those contentions.

Whenever Professor Zimbardo was asked what his experiment was about, he claimed that it was an exploration into what 'prisoners' would do to reclaim control of a situation in which their freedoms had been stripped from them. There was no hypothesis ... just a fishing expedition for data.

The people conducting the Stanford Prison Experiment had no idea how their project would turn out. If they did understand what might ensue from their project, they would either not have run the experiment at all or they would have not been surprised when things had to be shut down after five to six days.

Similarly, the individuals conducting the Philadelphia Constitution Experiment had no idea how their project would turn out. They wanted the power to try certain things – i.e., go on a fishing expedition for data that might confirm their speculations concerning democratic governance – and the deeply flawed ratification process provided them with the opportunity that they sought ... just as a deeply flawed system of ethical oversight (with respect to the sort of psychological experiments that should be given the green light) enabled Professor Zimbardo to have the opportunity and power to run with his ideas.

People suffered as a result of the Stanford Prison Experiment. People also have suffered as a result of the Philadelphia Constitution Experiment.

Blacks, Indians, women, poor people, Chinese immigrants (as well as many other immigrant groups), Japanese-American citizens, the disenfranchised, and blue-collar workers have all been abused by the system of governance put into play by the Philadelphia Constitution Experiment. The people conducting that experiment have known about such abuses, but like the individuals running the prisoner experiment, they have been too caught up in their own delusional systems to fully appreciate, or care about, what they were doing to other people.

The environment – both locally and internationally -- has been progressively degraded under the 'watchful' eye of the inheritors of the Philadelphia Constitution Experiment. In addition, millions of people in other parts of the world have been slaughtered, their lands confiscated, and their resources plundered in order to keep the Philadelphia Constitution Experiment running ... just as young male subjects had to be abused in order to keep the Stanford Prisoner Experiment going.

Professor Zimbardo utilized various experts – in the form of prison consultants, a prison chaplain, and people who conducted various psychological tests and interviews – to help inform the manner in which his experiment was conducted. None of those experts prevented what transpired. In fact, in many ways such expertise merely helped color the delusional character of the understanding through which they perceived their experiment.

Similarly, the people who started running the Philadelphia Constitutional Experiment – as well as their subsequent successors – employed lawyers, leaders of various descriptions, economists, media experts, educators, corporate and business executives, bankers, and military strategists. Yet, none of this expertise prevented the abuse that is continuing to be perpetrated through the legacy of the Philadelphia Constitution Experiment.

Like the Stanford Prison Experiment, the people conducting the Philadelphia Constitution Experiment know that pathological things were happening within the context of their experimental operation. However, just as the people conducting the prison project decided that they had to manage the perception of the 'visitors' to their prison, the individuals handling the constitutional project also have decided they must take 'situational control' and, as a result, they lie to people and hide things from the 'outsiders' who come to them and are concerned about what is taking place within the context of the constitutional experiment.

The people who conducted the prisoner experiment had sufficient awareness to understand that if the parents and friends of the 'prisoners' were to find out about the actual abusive character of the experiment, they would pull their loved ones from the experiment. As a result, they set about trying to mask the odor of corruption that had crept into their experiment, as well as attempted to clean up the physical appearance the facilities and the 'prisoners.'

The people conducting the Philadelphia Constitution Experiment also have sufficient awareness to understand that if 'We the People' were to find out about the actual abusive nature of the constitutional experiment, the people would pull out of that project. As a result, the people conducting the Philadelphia Constitution Experiment spend a great deal of time, energy and resources attempting to mislead, misinform, and spread disinformation among 'We the People' with respect to the 'state of the nation.'

Just as keeping the Stanford Prisoner Experiment going was more important to the individuals conducting that project than was the physical and mental welfare of the 'subjects' participating in their experiment, so too, keeping the Philadelphia Constitution Experiment going is more important to the people running that experiment than is the physical and emotional well-being of the 'subjects' – i.e., 'We the People' – who have been induced to participate in the constitutional experiment.

The people who conducted the prisoner experiment were so caught up in their own delusions concerning what they believed was transpiring in their experiment, that they argued with any 'outsider' – and there was only one such 'outsider' -- who was permitted to peek behind the curtain of secrecy surrounding the experiment and expressed shock with respect to what was taking place. The 'outsider' was told that she didn't have what it takes to be a psychologist, and the 'outsider' was told about the groundbreaking research that was going on and how no one had ever witnessed

223

what was taking place within their experiment, and the 'outsider' was told that no one who been a witness to what was transpiring within the 'prison' had objected to what was taking place.

Similarly, the people conducting the constitutional experiment are so caught up in their own delusions concerning what they believe is transpiring within the context of their experiment, that they argue with and ridicule any 'outsider' who comes along and, somehow, gets to look behind the 'wizard's curtain,' and, as a result, begins to take issue with what is transpiring there. Such 'outsiders' are told that the constitutional project is the greatest experiment the world has ever known, and the 'outsider' is told that groundbreaking, breathtaking progress has been achieved because of that experiment – the sort of progress that the world has never before witnessed – and the 'outsider' is told that no one who has witnesses what is transpiring within the constitutional experiment has ever objected to what was taking place there.

To those 'outsiders' who are able to witness the tremendous abuses that are taking place within the context of the constitutional experiment and as a result of that project, such arguments are nothing more than attempts to rationalize the indefensible. If people have to be abused in order for progress to be achieved, then there is something inherently pathological about that notion of progress.

Unfortunately, the people conducting the constitutional experiment are too entangled in their own delusional thinking in relation to their project to understand that they don't have the right to abuse people ... any more than the individuals running the prisoner experiment had a right to abuse their subjects in order to serve the purposes of that project. There is no justification concerning those experiments that can demonstrate beyond a reasonable doubt that abusing people is okay and, therefore, the individuals conducting the experiment should be permitted to continue on with their pathological activities.

The individuals conducting the prisoner experiment might have had the most noble of intentions when they began their project. Similarly, the individuals conducting the constitutional experiment might have had the most noble of intentions when they began their project.

None of the foregoing matters because irrespective of whether the people conducting the respective experiments understood it or not, their intentions – noble though they might be -- led to the deliberate abuse of other human beings. Moreover, when those abuses were brought to their attention, they retreated into various delusional systems of thought in order to justify to themselves that the abuses that were occurring as a result of their grand experiments were something other than what they were.

Whether by design or out of denial, Professor Zimbardo and other staff members in the Stanford Prisoner Experiment lied to the 'prisoners' and told the 'prisoners' that their troubles were of their own making. The people conducting the experiment had ample evidence on video and audio tape, as well as through their own direct observations, that not only were the 'guards' behaving in ways that were not permitted by the contractual conditions governing the prisoner experiment, but as well, the 'guards' were inventing reasons and justifications for punishing the prisoners in ways that were disproportionate to anything done by the 'prisoners.'

Similarly, whether by design or out of denial, the people running the constitutional experiment have lied again and again to 'We the People' and have sought to justify such lying by claiming that the people are the authors of their own misfortune. For instance, those who, over the years, have conducted the constitutional experiment have set forth a mythology (a mythology rooted in misinformation and disinformation of one kind or another) which claims that: It was necessary for the Philadelphia Convention to be secretive and for everyone but the would-be architects of the propose constitution to be kept away from the experiment in constitution-making, and it was necessary for the participants in the Philadelphia Convention to disregard the wishes of the Continental Congress, as well as the provisions of the Articles of Confederation, and it was necessary to induce the members of the Continental Congress to be derelict in their duties under The Articles of Confederation, and it was necessary for the states to be derelict in their duties under The Articles of Confederation, and that it was necessary for many facets of the ratification process to be rigged in favor of those who supported the idea of adopting the Philadelphia Constitution, and that it was necessary for the flawed ratification process to be imposed on people, and that it was necessary for everyone to feel obligated in relation to the results of such a process ... and that whatever abuses have transpired in the context of such a constitutional experiment are entirely the fault of 'We the People' and has nothing to do with the structural character of the constitutional experiment and has nothing to do with the pathological conduct of the people who are overseeing that project.

The people conducting the Stanford Prisoner Experiment claimed that experiment was about what steps the 'prisoners' would take to reclaim their sense of personal agency after, or while, they were made to feel powerless through the actions of the 'guards'. The individuals running the prisoner experiment went to considerable lengths to enable the 'guards' to abuse the 'prisoners' ... even to the extent of permitting the 'guards' to continuously push the envelope on the issue of physical violence despite the fact that the 'guards' were contractually obligated to observe the rule concerning no physical violence.

The individuals conducting the Philadelphia Constitutional Experiment claim that their experiment is about self-governance – that is, the co-operative exercise of the sense of personal agency of 'We the People' – and the constitutional experiment is about what 'We the People' (i.e., the subjects) will do once constitutional arrangements have been made to make 'We the People' feel as powerless as possible through the actions of the Executive, Congress, the Judiciary, and the state. In addition, the people running the constitutional experiment have gone to considerable lengths to enable the constitutional system to abuse 'We the People' … even to the extent of letting the 'guardians' of the government continuously push the envelope with respect to violating their contractual obligations concerning the 'rights' of 'We the People' in relation to, among other things, the issue of self-governance.

Just as the individuals running the Stanford Prisoner Experiment told their experimental subjects that they would have the right to withdraw from the experiment at any time, so too, the people conducting the constitutional experiment point to the Declaration of Independence and indicate how that document addresses the right of the people to abolish governments that are not serving the proper ends of governance. Moreover, just as the people running the prisoner experiment sought to manipulate their 'prisoners' when the latter individuals sought release from the prisoner experiment, so too, the individuals conducting the constitutional experiment manipulate 'We the People' by indicating that with respect to the basic issues of governance, "you can check out any time you like, but you can never leave" – *'Hotel California,'* The Eagles.

The people conducting the Stanford Prisoner Experiment claimed that they were the most qualified, objective individuals to evaluate what was taking place in their experiment. Yet, they didn't have a clue what they were doing, for if they did, the experiment would not have been terminated eight days earlier than scheduled.

The people who initiated the Philadelphia Constitution Experiment claimed that they are the most qualified, 'disinterested,' republican individuals to judge the character of their experiment. Nevertheless, within ten years of the inception of that experiment, people such as Madison and Hamilton who had been allies throughout the Philadelphia Convention, as well as during the ratification process (in the latter case, they, among other case, wrote the vast majority of the essays that would become *The Federalist Papers*), turned into the sort of enemies they might never have considered possible a few years earlier.

Such transformational shifts are suggestive. They indicate that one, or more, of the two aforementioned individuals didn't necessarily understand the nature of the experiment they had set in motion.

Professor Zimbardo's romantic partner broke with him over the prisoner experiment and couldn't understand how the person she believed she loved could permit such abusive things to happen to his subjects. Professor Zimbardo belittled his romantic partner and questioned her capacity for objectivity and research

Similarly, although Madison and Hamilton were not romantically involved, nonetheless, as fellow overseers of the constitutional experiment, each of them, in his own way, could not understand what had come over their former traveling companion along the path of republicanism. They soon were belittling one another in relation to the manner in which they respectively considered the other person to be guilty of betraying the principles of the Philadelphia Constitution Experiment ... despite the fact that the principles of that document were never actually justified beyond a reasonable doubt -- not even to individuals participating in the Philadelphia Convention given that they all had agreed there were many problems inherent in the constitutional experiment they had devised, and given that at least six individuals (George Mason, Elbridge Gerry, Edmond Randolph, John Lansing, Jr., Robert Yates, and Luther Martin) rejected what was transpiring in the Philadelphia Convention.

The people conducting the Stanford Prisoner Experiment induced the subjects who would become 'prisoners' to cede their sense of personal agency to the individuals running the project. Out of a sense of trust – along with other motivations – the subjects who were to become 'prisoners' did cede their sense of personal agency to the people conducting the experiment.

The people overseeing the prisoner project permitted the 'guards' to have an enhanced sense of personal agency by permitting them to have physical and emotional authority over, and control of, the 'prisoners.' In order to accomplish this, the individuals conducting the experiment had to cede some of their own agency – after all, they were the ones who supposedly were running the experiment – to the 'guards.'

Once enabled in the foregoing fashion, the guards – or, at least, some of them -- leveraged the agency that had been ceded to them by the experimenters and set about abusing the 'prisoners,' and began to push the envelope with respect to the rule which indicated that physical violence could not be used in the 'prison' by either the 'guards' or the 'prisoners.' Thereafter, the violent activities of the 'guards' were re-cast by the experimenters as something other than the abuse and contractual violations that they actually were.

The sorts of things that have noted above also have taken place -- and are continuing to occur -- in relation to the Philadelphia Constitution Experiment. The provisions of the Philadelphia Constitution – as interpreted by the Executive, the Judiciary, Congress, and the states -- have been used to induce the ceding of an enhanced sense of personal agency to the 'guardians' of the constitutional experiment ... which, unfortunately, happens to be the: Executive, Judiciary, Congress, and states, and, therefore, contrary to the principles of republicanism, they all have become judges in their own causes.

Once enabled in the foregoing fashion, the 'guardians' of the experiment in democracy have proceeded to leverage the power that has been ceded to them through elections. As a result -- and as was true in the prisoner experiment -- the constitutional 'guardians' began – almost from the outset of the constitutional experiment -- to treat the 'prisoners' (i.e., We the People) in arbitrary and abusive ways as those 'guardians' sought to push the envelope with respect to violating the rights of the people in relation to the issue of self-governance – that is, the co-operative exercise of their sense of collective and individual personal agency.

The word "arbitrary" is used in the previous sentence because whether one is talking about the Executive, the Judicial, the Congressional, or the state branches of government, none of these facets of governance has been able to demonstrate beyond a reasonable doubt that their respective interpretations of the Philadelphia Constitution are viable ways of serving the purposes and principles that were set forth in the Preamble to the Constitution, or that their interpretation of governance can be justified, beyond a reasonable doubt, with respect to the 'original right' to which Justice Marshall referred in *Marbury v. Madison.* Consequently, the very fact of the arbitrariness surrounding those interpretive activities makes them abusive in relation to each human being's basic right of sovereignty – that is, the right to have a fair opportunity to push back the horizons of ignorance with respect to the nature of reality. Any interference with that sort of sovereignty that cannot be justified beyond a reasonable doubt is arbitrary.

In the Stanford Prisoner Experiment, the behaviors of the 'guards' and the 'prisoners' are said to give expression to the manner in which situational forces come to dominate the dispositional tendencies of individuals, thereby, inducing individuals to behave in ways that would not otherwise occur. Entirely left out of the foregoing account is the manner in which the people running the experiment manipulated the sense of personal agency of both the 'guards' as well as the 'prisoners' and, in addition, ceded their own sense of personal agency to the kind of delusional understanding of the experiment that would permit fundamental violations of the contractual rules supposedly governing the experiment to occur in order to keep the experiment going.

In the Philadelphia Constitution Experiment, the behaviors of the 'guardians' of democracy are said to give expression to the manner in which the situational principles of the Constitution come to dominate the dispositional tendencies of individuals, thereby enabling individuals to behave in 'civilized' and 'democratic' ways that would not otherwise occur. Entirely left out of that kind of an account is the manner in which the people running the constitutional experiment have manipulated the sense of personal agency of the 'prisoners' (i.e., We the People) and induced them to cede such agency to the 'guardians' of democracy who, then, proceed to leverage that power to serve their own delusional understanding concerning: 'sovereignty,' rights,' 'justice,' 'liberty,' 'welfare,' 'tranquility,' and the 'common defense.'

Finally, during the Stanford Prisoner Experiment, there came a point during their project in which the individuals conducting the experiment convinced themselves that one of the 'prisoners' whom they had permitted to be abused and, then, subsequently released was going to come back with a gang of friends and free the remaining 'prisoners' as well as trash the 'prison.' They became so obsessed with the idea that they sought to move their experiment to an 'out of use' jail facility outside of the university, and when this plan did not work out, moved all the 'prisoners' to a windowless, poorly ventilated storage facility for three hours in order to foil the fiendish plans of the former 'prisoner.'

The foregoing delusional fantasy was set in motion by: (1) several 'guards' claiming that they heard the 'prisoners' talking about such a plot, and (2) one of the 'guards' claiming that he had seen the released 'prisoner' skulking about the halls of the Psychology Department. Rather than investigating to determine whether, or not, there was any truth to the various allegations of the 'guards', the experimenters entered into a paranoid delusional state and took steps that were consistent with such a condition – that is, they did what they thought was necessary to preserve their own experiment no matter how it might affect the 'prisoners.'

Eventually, the experimenters returned the 'prisoners' to the 'prison' facility in the basement. The had come to the conclusion that the whole 'plot' was nothing but 'rumor,' and failed to understand that their behavior was a function of delusional thinking that was present long before the 'rumors' surfaced and that the 'rumors' had been given credence because they were filtered through the lenses of a delusional system of thinking.

Similarly, the 'guardians' of democracy tend to operate out of a delusional framework that is based on arbitrary and abusive interpretations of the Constitution that often compels them to filter unsubstantiated rumors – for example, those connected with Afghanistan in 2001, or those connected with Iraq in 2003, or those connected with Vietnam in the 1960s – through such delusional thinking in a way that has (and has had) terrible consequences for many people ... both Americans and people elsewhere in the world. Furthermore, the purpose underlying those exercises of paranoid delusions is not to protect the 'prisoners' (i.e., We the People') but, instead, is directed toward keeping the experiment going in a fashion that will permit that project to remain completely under the control of those who are conducting the constitutional experiment while operating out of a delusional framework concerning the sovereignty of the 'prisoners' (i.e., We the People') that they are abusing in arbitrary ways ... that is, in ways that cannot be justified.

About 19 years ago, a book entitled: *The Guru Papers*, by Joel Kramer & Diana Alstad, made quite a splash in many circles. The sub-title of the work was: *Masks of Authoritarian Power*.

The following comments serve as something of an extended mini-review of the foregoing work. In this review, a substantial amount of time is given to providing readers with what I consider to be a fair and accurate overview of the perspective of the two authors, but toward the end of this essay, a certain amount of critical analysis concerning their work is provided, so please be patient.

One of the essential themes of the Kramer - Alstad study was that all Guru-devotee or teacher-seeker relationships are inherently, unavoidably, irrevocably, problematically, and without exception, authoritarian in nature. Although the authors knew most about the way things worked in Yogic and Buddhist systems, the two writers were quite clear that they believed no spiritual, mystical tradition was free from the destructive presence of authoritarian practices and influences.

Furthermore, these two authors argued that no one should suppose the central difficulty in such teacher-seeker relationships could be attributed to the personal failings of a few rotten apples in the barrel -- that is, Kramer and Alstad maintained that even if one could remove from consideration all those teachers who had given in to the dark side of themselves and, as a result, became abusers and exploiters of their followers, nevertheless, the remaining spiritual guides -- no matter how good, decent, well-intended, and knowledgeable they might be -- would still be ensconced in a system that was inextricably authoritarian. In other words, the problem was institutional or systemic and not a function of wayward and rogue 'teachers'. Even when the individual apples were good, the barrel in which they existed and operated was rotten with the insidious presence of authoritarian practices.

Early in *The Guru Papers*, the two authors made a distinction between, on the one hand, issues of authority, as well as hierarchy, and, on the other hand, authoritarian practices that are often confused and conflated with the former two principles. According to Kramer and Alstad, every society or social order requires the use of authority and hierarchy to be able to function properly, but when authoritarian influences seep into either the uses of authority or hierarchy, then, according to the authors, the seeds of eventual social disintegration are being sown.

While Kramer and Alstad are interested in a wide variety of social contexts that tend to become entangled with authoritarian abuses, the two researchers key in on spiritual, religious, and mystical contexts because such traditional settings offer, in their opinion, an unusually fruitful opportunity to explore the way the absolutist nature of the Guru-seeker relationship is rooted, supposedly, in demands for total obedience and surrender, and, consequently, provides a window, as it were, onto the manner in which the exercise of authoritarian power leads to not only the control of physical contingencies, but to the shaping, structuring, coloring, and orienting of mental, emotional, motivational, and behavioral processes, as well.

According to the perspective of the authors of *The Guru Papers*, spiritual ideologies are used in authoritarian systems to, among other things, justify and render plausible, or reasonable, the exercise of authoritarian control. When one accepts a spiritual system, one, knowingly or unknowingly, commits oneself to submitting to whatever yoke of authoritarian power the system deems to be appropriate in order to enable the spiritual institution, in question, to operate smoothly, efficiently, and effectively as a means of -- so the promise goes -- helping individuals to become: realized, enlightened, fully human, awakened, saved, sanctified, or whatever other spiritual ideals are being promulgated by that spiritual system as being the goal(s) or purpose(s) of life.

Kramer and Alstad claim to have no quarrel with the idea of spirituality, per se. Rather, their stated concern is with processes that seek to justify, defend, enhance, promote, and/or mask the exercise of authoritarian control by creating gateway figures -- i.e., teachers, gurus, masters --

who, allegedly, are the only ones who can safely and effectively guide one to the spiritual treasures on the other side of the spiritual gate -- even when that gate resides within us -- and do so by requiring followers to refrain from challenging, in any way, the guide's directives, interpretations, pronouncements, practices, demands, expectations, or understandings.

The two authors believe the vast majority of historical, traditional, social systems are saturated with the uses, and subsequent destructive effects, of authoritarian power. They feel the omnipresence of such practices and influences has undermined our individual and collective capacity for self-trust, and this, in turn, has shackled our creative potential for developing new social and institutional arrangements concerning constructive uses of authority and hierarchy that are capable of solving the many dilemmas with which we are confronted.

The creators of *The Guru Papers* are in search of a new paradigm -- one that will attract commitment through consensus rather than the coercive force inherent in authoritarian demands for mental, social, spiritual, emotional and physical obedience, submission, or conformity. The authors are seeking a paradigm shift that will give emphasis to helping people to learn how to trust and value their own experiences rather than succumbing to a rote-learning process of indoctrination fraught with unexamined assumptions, as well as a submissive compulsion to blindly follow antiquated, problematic value and methodological systems.

Of particular interest to Kramer and Alstad are the techniques used by authoritarian systems to inculcate a set of moral values that are internalized and used to control people. According to the authors, such techniques are even more important than the exercise of physical control, for the latter is quite limited in scope and cannot be used on a continuous basis without either, sooner or later, leading to social upheaval and significant challenges through some form of countervailing physical force, or simply leading to the fragmentation of society as the pressure of physical force generates ruptures in the social fabric that are unpredictable and, often, irreparable.

When authoritarian processes are used to shape how people think, believe, feel, speak, and act, the world-view, paradigm, or framework through which reality is engaged and understood becomes the medium of control. The most dangerous shackles are the ones that are invisible to us because we do not see them for what they are -- namely, authoritarian demands for obedience that have been internalized and re-framed as unchallengeable moral certitudes that are justified by an ideology one has been induced not to question or critically reflect upon.

Moreover, from the perspective of Kramer and Alstad, one of the primary functions of encouraging the idea of moral certainty in people is that the latter instills in the minds of such individuals a self-righteous attitude that justifies perpetrating all manner of cruelty, hatred, anger, and oppression toward the 'miscreants' who have not, yet, submitted to such 'truths' and, therefore, serves as the ideological warrant for telling other people -- by force, if necessary -- how to live their lives, what goals to seek, which authorities to believe or trust, who to be and why. The sort of certitude that is indifferent to facts, evidence, critical analysis, contrary experience, unbiased evaluation, methodological rigor, unexplained anomalies, unanswered questions, and soulful reflection is impervious to anything other than its own interests, likes, dislikes, prejudices, goals, assumptions, and limitations.

Such rigidity and dogmatic impenetrability is used as the first line of defense against any challenges to the moral justification for perpetrating a system that is, essentially, operated through authoritarian processes that, ultimately, demand total obedience and submission to the purveyors of the oppressive practices that have been used to indoctrinate people to accept such a moral, emotional, mental, and spiritual cul-de-sac or dead end in the first place. The system is circular, and, therefore, self-perpetuating as long as the underlying authoritarian practices enjoy the privileges of eminent domain that are assumed to be absolute, and, therefore, unchallengeable by virtue of the moral certitude that, supposedly, lies at the heart of the assumption that is vouchsafing those privileges and that, consequently, underwrites the justification for doing things in an authoritarian fashion.

According to the authors of *The Guru Papers*, morality is the mortar that cements the bricks of society together, and in order to avoid the appearance of requiring people to abide by arbitrarily derived rules of conduct, morality was embedded in religious systems that were, in turn, backed by claims to the ultimate authority of absolute truths that were Divine in nature. Thus, morality, religion, spirituality, goodness, justice, meaning, purpose, community, and identity all took their lead from a set of Divinely given absolute principles.

Kramer and Alstad contend that central to the aforementioned set of principles was a 'renunciate' orientation to life. This r enunciate philosophy or theology required individuals to sacrifice self-interest in the name of the 'higher good' as defined by a given religious framework and as interpreted by those who came to be the guardians of that system -- namely, the spiritual guides, clerics, officials, and so on, who, supposedly, were most knowledgeable about what Divinity wanted from humankind.

The two authors further argued that forgiveness, guilt, reward, shame, and punishment were among the primary tools used to induce people to adopt the renunciate perspective and eschew self-interest. In fact, the guardians of these spiritual frameworks pointed out that real self-interest was synonymous with adhering to a renunciate way of life -- that, in effect, there was no essential antagonism between the two.

Issues of death, life, loss, pain, purpose, meaning, difficulty, uncertainty, the unknown, were dealt with through the fixed symbols, myths, rituals, and mysteries of absolute truth. However, Kramer and Alstad maintain that the price for pushing back the apparent chaos of life-events in this fashion was a way of being that became anachronistic due to its inability to flexibly, reasonably, creatively, and effectively respond to the challenges and problems generated through on-going history.

Under the relentless pressure of history, the authors contend that many of the myths, symbols, and rituals have been disconnected from their original sources, and, consequently, there has been a wide -spread loss of an essential sense of meaning, purpose, identity, and community that has led to considerable moral decay as people no longer see the relevance of abiding by renunciate theologies that do not seem to serve either collective or individual well-being. This state of affairs has, in the view of Kramer and Alstad, led to the rise of various forms of fundamentalism that seek to, ever more tightly, cling to traditional -- or, what are believed to be traditional - values, methods, beliefs, and practices in an attempt to revive, through an exercise of sheer intensity of will-power, what seems to have been lost ... as if the mere urgency and direness of human desperation could turn back the calendar to a simpler, seemingly more innocent and spiritually advantageous time.

In the view of the authors of *The Guru Papers*, fundamentalists are experiencing a loss of control over their lives. They feel powerless in the face of modern forms of science, technology, culture, communication, government, education, and economics that have leveraged power in ways that bring traditional modes of spiritual life under constant attack, generating many doubts and questions in the process, and, as well, create an onslaught of moral problems for traditionally minded and hearted individuals.

Kramer and Alstad believe that what is needed at this juncture of history is "an ethics for survival". In their opinion, renunciate systems focus on rewards and punishments in a world-to-come context that looks upon existence from a self-serving paradigm that favors authoritarian means as a way of serving such ends, and, therefore, do little but use tactics of fear and self-righteous anger to force people to submit to a system that does very little to solve the problems and eliminate the injustices of the present world.

The authors contend that renunciate systems of morality are inherently judgmental and use fear and force to impose this perspective on people. In other words, individuals become so imbued with the fear of bringing down upon themselves the wrath of God or of being denied the fruits of Heaven -- at least, according to the teachings of the guardians of the faith -- that the commonality of people often become paralyzed with indecision ... not wishing to do anything that will jeopardize their standing in eternity, and, in the process, helping to perpetuate an authoritarian approach to life that spreads destructive seeds everywhere it blows.

Kramer and Alstad believe that the spirit of the authoritarian mind-set is nowhere more apparent than in mystical systems that are based on a teacher-seeker relationship in which a seeker blindly concedes authority to another person who claims to be a spiritual guide, and, in the process of such a concession, a number of untested and unproven assumptions are made concerning the character, understanding, and authenticity of the so-called teacher. Such a seeker is operating on presuppositions such as: the 'teacher' is morally superior to the seeker, and, as well, enjoys a far greater degree of spiritual knowledge, self-realization, insight, potential, and closeness to Divinity, than the seeker does -- all of which supposedly enables the 'teacher' to understand what is best for another individual.

In the opinion of Kramer and Alstad, the foregoing sorts of presuppositions lend themselves to the creation of different forms of dualism, and among the most important of these is the sacred and non-sacred dichotomy. In the context of the teacher-seeker relationship, whatever the teacher is, says, thinks, feels, does, indicates, and suggests is sacred, and whatever is not in consonance with these dimensions of the teacher is non-sacred.

The task of the seeker becomes one of absorbing or of activating this sense of sacredness within herself or himself and, in addition, eliminating the non-sacred. The task of the teacher is to assist the seeker to do this.

As such, the teacher becomes the role model through which this is to be accomplished. However, the authors of *The Guru Papers* feel that much of what is passed off as sacred in such mystical circles is little more than vested interests, self-aggrandizement, cultural constructions, and individual preferences on the part of the 'teacher'.

When the 'teacher' becomes the unchallengeable arbiter of truth and 'seekers' adopt renunciate methodologies and moralities that encourage the latter to sacrifice their own capacity for experience, reflection, analysis, questioning, exploration, trust, identity, and realization at the altar of a teacher, then, in the opinion of Kramer and Alstad, one has an authoritarian recipe for spiritual disaster that is likely to produce little more than people who are dogmatic, rigid, static, self-righteous, judgmental, elitist, as well as incapable of either thinking for themselves or trusting their inner selves.

The Guru Papers approaches the issues of authoritarian power through the spectacles of a broadly evolutionary, progressive, humanistic, rationalistic, dialectical point of view. Although I believe the authors have some good insights to offer with respect to a number of the problems that exist in many teacher-seeker relationships (both on the side of the guide, as well as on the side of the seeker), nonetheless, their overall analysis appears to suffer from many inadequacies, lacunae, presumptions, unanswered questions, and problems -- not the least of which is the entirely arbitrary nature of their conception of dialectical analysis, rationalistic methodology, and moral valuation, in addition to the constant vagueness in their book that dogs such key issues as: authority, hierarchy, self, trust, spirituality, creativity, evolution, truth, abstraction, purpose, identity, enlightenment, love and knowledge.

The Guru Papers is more than 370 pages long and, perhaps, at least that many pages might be necessary to demonstrate that the authors have not proven their central thesis that the nature of the teacher-seeker relationship is necessarily authoritarian. I am -- as I believe many people would be -- quite prepared to concede that, all too frequently, such relationships are riddled with authoritarian practices and influences, but claiming that such practices and influences are systemic and unavoidable in these sorts of relationship is quite another matter. In my view, the authors certainly have not proven their central thesis beyond a reasonable doubt, and, moreover, I do not believe they even have met a far less stringent burden of proof that requires them to have demonstrated that their thesis, on the basis of a preponderance of evidence, is likely true -- in other words, that the teacher-seeker relationship is necessarily authoritarian in nature.

There are a number of comments that could be made in defense of the foregoing critical pronouncements concerning *The Guru Papers*. But, rather than occupy the reader's time with the long version of such comments, I will only note a few possibilities.

To begin with, demanding or expecting that Being should be reducible to rationalistic methodologies -- as Kramer and Alstad tend to do -- is not only arbitrary and not amenable to proof, but it is, essentially, authoritarian in scope and principle. Moreover, such a position presupposes there is a consensus of opinion about what constitutes the rational or the logical, when, in truth, none exists.

This is not to say there is no such thing as logic or rational methodology, but, rather, it is a reflection of the reality that there are a variety of modalities of rational and logical processes about which much critical discussion has taken place. Differences in philosophy, science, theology, law, literature, culture, linguistics, education, and mysticism all testify to the fact that there is an on-going search for the logical, the rational, and the commonsensical in everyday life.

Point-counterpoint-point-counterpoint is the rhythm of intellectual life. The tapestry woven by various rational techniques produces an intriguing but chaotic set of antagonistic motifs in our individual and collective minds.

Where is the truth in all of this? What is its significance? How do we use it to identify the real?

Furthermore, there are forms of understanding with which we are all familiar that resist, if not defy, rational, logical analysis in many ways. There is an intelligence to seeing, hearing, feeling, being, and consciousness, which does not seem reducible to any discernible scheme of rational, logical discourse. Maybe, in the future this might all change, but, right now, reason and logic have not been able to fathom the mysteries that envelop our existence and through which we engage such existence.

The very nature of the mystical way is that it is said to be ineffable. Yes, all kinds of people have written whole libraries about the contexts surrounding the ineffable, but the unspoken and unspeakable remain what they are -- secrets that, to whatever extent they can be grasped, are best engaged through the trans-rational realms of venues such as the heart, spirit, and Self.

One can agree with Kramer and Alstad that one should not pursue the mystical way naively, blindly, unquestioningly, mechanically, and without rational reflection. However, there are many times on the spiritual path when rational analysis will not provide one with definitive, certain, unchallengeable answers -- not unless we wish to make reason an authoritarian force within us that is absolute and that cannot be questioned as to its reliability, validity, potential, and limitations.

There are many aspects of life, many experiences, for which reason has not even the foggiest of plausible explanations for how they are possible. Consciousness, creativity, talent, language, logic, intelligence, and rationality are just a few of these unknown facts of life.

Many rationalists would like to reduce faith down to belief but balk when they realize that, from such a perspective, having faith in rationality becomes little more than an exercise in generating a belief system about the nature of thought. Faith is far more complex than mere belief, and, as a result, faith leads into unchartered territories, where the sextant of rationalism and the known charts of logic do not always help one find one's way in the darkness of existence.

We live in the midst of uncertainty, ignorance, ambiguity, possibility, antagonistic forces, and need. As a result, we are vulnerable.

We require someone to show us how to supplement and complement rational tools with other modalities of knowing and understanding. We need someone to initiate us into a process of

being able to have a constructive dialectic between
reason and the trans-rational.

252

Kramer and Alstad are smart, talented, articulate, serious explorers. Yet, I know they don't know how to do the foregoing. This is obvious -- both from what they say, as well as from what they don't say.

The authors tell me to trust myself, but they don't provide any solid clues about who the self is that I am supposed to trust. More importantly, they aren't very clear about why I should trust this mysterious 'self' to which they allude in their book.

What is this 'self' rooted in? -- The truth? -- Reality in some sense of this word? How do we know this? How can we be certain of this? Is this 'self' absolute and unchallengeable? Where did this 'self' come from? What is its purpose, or does it have any? Is this self a 'rational' self? -- A transpersonal 'self'? Is this 'self' solipsistic and the creator of reality? If so, how does it accomplish this? What values should this 'self' live or judge by? How are these values derived? Why should one trust the method of derivation? What is the significance of experience? Are they arbitrary or do they have a meaning, and, if so, what is that meaning, and how do we discover the nature of such meaning? What methods should be used? What happens when this 'self' comes into conflict or disagreement with other 'selves'? How should disputes be resolved? Why? How does one address all of the foregoing without slipping into authoritarian practices?

The authors of *The Guru Papers* have a theory about all of the foregoing, but that is all it is -- an untested, unproven, problematic, ambiguous, vague, incomplete theory. It is a world-view, a paradigm, a philosophical framework -- a framework that cannot offer me one, incontestable, definitive smoking-gun of a reason why one should adopt their perspective ... other than, of course, the obvious fact that there seem to be problems everywhere else in the arena of rational discourse, and, so, why not try 'our' (i.e., their) way of doing things.

Beyond the foregoing issues, I think that Kramer and Alstad have made a mistake in reasoning that is quite similar to one that Freud, among many others, made. More specifically, one is on shaky ground when one tries to construct a model of healthy relationships based on an exploration of pathology.

In other words, the authors of *The Guru Papers* go into a great deal of detail about teacher-seeker relationships that have gone wrong, together with the difficulties that arise out of such dysfunctional relationships -- both for individuals and society. One can agree with a great deal that they have to say in this respect.

Nevertheless, they are using an inductive variation of extrapolation which implies that because some -- or even many -- teacher-seeker relationships are diseased, then, all such relationships must be diseased and, moreover, that all teacher-seeker relationships must necessarily manifest the same debilitating set of processes from which there is no escape. However, if what they were saying were actually true, then, the relationship that any reader has with their book must be inherently dysfunctional and, consequently, doomed to failure because the general format of this sort of relationship is that of someone who is imparting a version of reality/truth to someone who is interested in seeking after the nature of reality/truth -- that is, loosely construed, a teacher-seeker relationship.

The authors might counter with something along the following lines. Precisely because we do not commit any of the mistakes present in problematic guru-devotee relationships, we have provided a healthy, constructive opportunity to explore issues, ideas, problems, and so on that is free from authoritarian influences and practices. The presumptuousness of such a riposte -- if it were to happen -- is in the belief that a spiritual guide could not accomplish what the authors have been able to pull off -- or, so, the latter might believe.

Kramer and Alstad want to help readers develop a sense of trust in their inner selves. They wish to do this without force, compulsion, trickery, deceit, duplicity, insincerity, manipulation, exploitation, dishonesty. They wish to achieve this through a reciprocity with, and respect for, the integrity and self-determining sovereignty of the other person.

The authors would like to have truth, facts, evidence, experience, and rigorous methodology decide such matters, rather than bias, prejudice, dogma, unexamined assumptions, conformity, and blind acceptance. Kramer and Alstad would like individuals to become free, autonomous, independent thinkers and doers who are interested in the welfare of all of Creation even as they strive to realize their own essential potential and unique identity.

The two writers would like people to reconcile and harmonize oppositions within themselves, as well as across all social relationships, by extending and expanding the notion of the sacred to include the whole of Being, and not just be restricted to the next-world and/or arbitrarily selected 'holy' people. The authors of *The Guru Papers* would like to establish modes of justice, decency, morality, and discernment that are not arrogant, narrow, self-serving, exclusionary attempts at justifying and perpetuating authoritarian systems of power.

Kramer and Alstad might be surprised to discover that there actually are spiritual, mystical guides who speak in the same sort of terms, goals, purposes, priorities intentions, and methods as do these authors. An authentic teacher -- of whatever kind -- is interested in only one thing ... assisting an individual to discover the truth about life, identity, capacity, justice, service, knowledge, community, love, self, integrity, freedom, realization, wisdom, as well as the nature of one's relationship with Being and the many levels and dimensions of manifested Creation.

An authentic teacher -- spiritual or otherwise -- does not want a student to become the teacher. Such teachers want a person to become herself or himself ... to realize his or her potential ... to come to know one's place in the scheme of things and to be freely committed to being all that one's capacity permits one to be.

An authentic teacher assists an individual to learn how, when, why, and where to trust herself or himself under different circumstances. Authentic teachers induce seekers to submit to the truth and to be satisfied with nothing less than the truth.

Over the last 40 years, or so, there have been two people in my life with whom I have had a teacher-seeker relationship. One of these was authentic, healthy, and constructive, while the other was not, but I learned from both sets of relationship.

If the sequence of life events had been reversed so that I had to endure the dysfunctional relationship first, I don't know how I might have responded to subsequent events -- including meeting up with someone who actually was an authentic spiritual guide. However, by the Grace of God, I didn't encounter the problematic relationship first, but instead I had a nonpathological relationship as my introduction to the mystical path. Many others have not been so fortunate.

I know from my own personal experience that Kramer and Alstad's thesis concerning the alleged inherent, authoritarian nature of all teacher-seeker relationships is wrong. My first -- and, so far, only authentic -- guide was the exact antithesis of an authoritarian. He never asked -- directly or indirectly -- for me to submit myself to him, or to conform to his ways of doing things, or to blindly and unquestioningly accept any of the things that he said or did. He was extremely humble and never even hinted at being superior to others. He permitted all manner of questions and was very generous in the time, resources, and efforts that he devoted to providing insights, principles, explanations, and teachings concerning various facets of spirituality -- both exoteric and esoteric. In fact, his way of doing things was, ultimately, by the Grace of God, my salvation in dealing with the very problematic ramifications of the spiritually dysfunctional 'teacher' with whom I later came into contact after my mystical guide passed away in the late 1980s.

The line of demarcation that differentiates between spiritual authenticity and a spiritual fraud can be very tricky to discern. Even when, on the surface, everything appears to be 'kosher', nevertheless, if someone is described as a bona fide spiritual guide who does things in a constructive, well-intentioned, non-authoritarian manner, and, yet, such a person has not been authorized by Divinity, then, such an individual is a spiritual fraud and cannot serve as the channel of transmission for the spiritual assistance that is necessary to traverse the mystical path, and, as a result, is placing people in harm's way -- both now, and, potentially, in the future -- even though, on the surface everything seems to be done with appropriate spiritual etiquette and with due diligence for the welfare of associated practitioners.

When minions of Satan appear in the manifested form of a Charlie Manson, Jim Jones, and so on, the decision seems clear cut -- although even here there were sincere people who were exploited. When the minions of Satan appear in the guise of a kindly, friendly, intelligent, charming, engaging, concerned, knowledgeable, passionate, committed teacher who claims spiritual authenticity where none exists, then, one has a real problem on one's hand, because once in the presence of the kind of spiritual quicksand in which the process of extrication might not be all that easy.

Among the chief reasons for such difficulty is that one often does not even realize one is dealing with a spiritual imposter, Indeed, beware of the arrogance that whispers to one's heart 'you could not make such an error', for it is happening every day among sincere people all over the world, and it is happening because we live in treacherous times where authentic spiritual light is very difficult to find and the forces of chaos, disinformation, and darkness are very prominent -- many of these forces call themselves spiritual guides and many people believe them.

The authentic teachers of mysticism often indicate that no one comes to Self-realization except through encountering both the compassionate and rigorous attributes of Divinity. I don't know what other, if any, rigorous, Divine attributes I will have to experience in my life as I continue my quest to learn how to serve the purpose of my existence, but there is no doubt in my mind, heart, and soul that a ten year period of my life -- the ones spent with a spiritual fraud -- have been very spiritually rigorous in character, for the relationship with the mystical imposter has entailed a great variety of difficulties ... difficulties that Divinity permitted, for there is no reality other than God, and difficulties that I am very thankful have, God willing, come to an end.

The Phenomenology of Charisma

Fifteen years ago (1997), Len Oakes, an Australian, wrote a book: *Prophetic Charisma: The Psychology of Revolutionary Personalities*. Building on the work of, among others, Max Weber and Heinz Kohut, as well as using insights gained through his personal experience with a cult-like group and leader, together with extensive psychological research involving testing, interviewing, and reading, Oakes sought to provide some degree of understanding and insight into the phenomenon of charisma.

While Oakes is to be commended for his attempt to bring light to an area that often exists in the shadows of our awareness, nevertheless, I feel his book is flawed in a number of essential ways. The following commentary constitutes some of my critical reflections upon Oakes' book.

The first problem I have is the manner in which Oakes approaches the idea of a 'prophet'. In order to understand the nature of the problem surrounding Oakes' use of the term 'prophet', his theory will have to be delineated somewhat.

To begin with, and as the aforementioned title indicates, Oakes engagement of charisma is through a psychological study and not from a religious or spiritual perspective. Therefore, one can acknowledge and appreciate that the way in which he defines the idea of a 'prophet' will be in a manner that is compatible with the psychological thrust of his study.

Notwithstanding the above acknowledgment, there are always advantages and disadvantages surrounding any choice one makes for a working or operational, definition of a given term. Consequently, one needs to determine if, how, and to what extent, Oakes's manner of defining key terms might introduce distortion and/or problems into his inquiry.

According to Oakes, a 'prophet' is characterized as anyone who: (a) proclaims a mission containing not just a recipe for salvation, but a mission that does so in a way that seeks to revolutionize conventional values; (b) draws, gathers, or attracts individuals who become followers of such an individual and seek to implement the guidance provided by the person being referred to as a 'prophet'. Oakes tends to lump together a number of people, ranging, on the one hand, from: Jesus and Muhammad, to: various Swamis, ministers, alternative community leaders, and the like.

Despite whatever differences might exist among those individuals to whom the label 'prophet' is given, Oakes suggest that what all of these individuals share in common are qualities such as: (1) a capacity to inspire people; (2) a resistance to, and opposition toward, various forms of conventionality; (3) possessing a remarkable and compelling personality that tends to set them apart from most people; (4) a grandiose sense of self-confidence that is the source for a great deal of optimism and fearlessness with respect to propagating the mission of salvation; (5) a natural capacity for acting that well-serves a 'prophet's tendency to manipulate people; (6) great rhetorical skills; (7) self-contained, independent of others, not given to self-disclosure; (8) a capacity for social insight that seems to border on the preternatural. Using the foregoing definition, Oakes identifies individuals such as: Joseph Smith, Madame Blavatsky, Bagwan Shree Rajneesh, Prabhupada Bhaktivedanta (Hare Khrishna), L. Ron Hubbard, Sun Myung Moon, and Jim Jones as instances of modern day 'prophets'.

Depending on how one understood the idea of 'salvation' in the above definition of 'prophet, one could expand the boundaries of the set of individuals who constitute 'prophets'. For example, Adolph Hitler, who many Germans saw as the salvation of the German people, could, on the basis of the stated definition, be considered a 'prophet' because he attracted people who sought to follow his guidance concerning the nature of life and, as well, because some dimensions of such guidance sought to revolutionize certain realms of conventional values -- and, in fact, Oakes discusses Hitler along these lines at various junctures in the former's book about charisma.

Oakes also lists Fritz Perls and Werner Erhard as exemplars of modern prophets. Since the sort of 'salvation' that Perls and Erhard sought for their clients does not easily, if at all, lend itself to spirituality, religion, or mysticism, then if individuals like Perls and Erhard are to be considered 'prophets' in Oakes' sense of the word, one also, potentially, might be able to apply that same definition to a great many other people besides Perls and Erhard who gave expression to various artistic, literary, philosophical, scientific, psychological, social, economic, and political theories. Indeed, consistent with Oakes' definition of a prophet, there are many personalities across history who developed theories and paradigms that were intended, in one way or another, to serve as ways to salvation, and who, in the process, proposed an overthrow of conventional values -- to one extent or another - - as necessary for a realization of salvation, and, finally, who attracted people who were interested in learning how to live their lives in accordance with the teachings of the 'master'.

Oakes borrows a distinction, made by Heinz Kohut -- a psychoanalyst -- between 'messianic' and 'charismatic' personalities in order to try to frame Oakes' way of approaching issues such as 'prophets', charisma, and narcissism. Among other things, this distinction lends a certain degree of specificity to the discussion of prophets and helps address the issue of why people such as Perls, Freud, Hitler, and Erhard are part of the same group as a variety of individuals who are oriented in a largely religious, spiritual, or mystical manner.

According to Oakes, messianic prophets as those who: (1) tend to identify God as an 'external' source of inspiration; (2) often interact with Divinity in terms of a personal relationship that has an 'objective' nature; (3) usually teach by means of revelation; (4) seem to be motivated by a fantasy that construes one's individual existence to be part of the Godhead; (5) are psychologically oriented toward the external world and, as a result, are able to perform reality checks; (6) frequently are described as being very consistent with respect to behaviors or beliefs and, therefore, are seen as stable over time; (7) are fairly modest with respect to making claims about themselves; (8) seek to do works of virtue and excellence in conjunction with the world, as well as seek to work for what is perceived to be the welfare of others; (9) apparently are resigned to experiencing an eventual decline in influence and, as a result, often willing to make preparations for transition in leadership; (10) tend to generate new laws that foster a form of release that, ultimately, serves as a source of helping to constrain society; (11) give emphasis to doing 'God's work' that is at the heart of the messianic mission; (12) are inclined to be other worldly and withdraw from the world's corrupting potential; (13) treat truth and duty to be the two highest forms of ethical expression.

On the other hand, for Oakes, charismatic prophets are those who: (1) locate Divinity within rather than externally (in contrast to what messianic prophets do); (2) filter their relationship

265

with 'being' in terms of impersonal forces; (3) teach by example rather than through revelation; (4) are motivated by the fantasy that 'I and the Godhead' are one; (5) tend to be out of touch with external reality and, therefore, unable to run reality checks; (6) are perceived as being inconsistent with respect to both beliefs and behaviors that leads to considerable instability over time; (7) are fairly immodest and given to bouts of self-aggrandizement; (8) are not interested in the welfare of others, but, rather, are likely to be antisocial and self-serving; (9) often self-destruct or fall from grace through their behaviors; (10) are oriented toward rebellion or a certain lawlessness, and consider release/freedom to be good in and of themselves; (11) seek recognition rather than seek to be a vehicle of God's work; (12) use the corruption of the world as a justification for amorality and the opportunistic exploitation of circumstances; (13) consider love and freedom to be the highest forms of ethical expression.

For the most part, Oakes considers messianic and charismatic types of prophets to constitute groups that are, to a large extent, mutually exclusive categories. In other words, if one compares the thirteen points outlined above in conjunction with both types of 'prophets', then with respect to whatever quality or characteristic is said to describe one type of 'prophet', there tends to be an absence of any common ground shared by members of the two, respective groups and, actually, in relation to any of the aforementioned thirteen characteristics, members of the two groups tend to be proceeding in very different directions -- sometimes in diametric opposition -- with respect to each of the points listed. Oakes does indicate that elements of each type of prophet might be combined in different sorts of permutations so that some individuals might give expression to mixed combinations of both messianic and charismatic types. However, on the whole, Oakes seems to believe that in most cases one can identify a given 'prophet' as being either of a messianic kind or a charismatic kind.

Although, as noted above, Oakes alludes to the possibility that a given individual might give expression to qualities and characteristics from each of the two sets of characteristics, he doesn't pursue this possibility in any concrete manner. Consequently, one doesn't really know what he means by his allusion other than that he states it as a possibility.

One could imagine someone who teaches by example (a charismatic trait) as well as through revelation (a messianic characteristic). In addition, one could conceive of an individual who located Divinity both within (a charismatic tendency) and without (a messianic quality). One also can acknowledge the possibility of there being 'leaders' who did not focus on just love and freedom (a charismatic property) or on just truth and duty (a messianic feature) but on all of these qualities together ... that is, love, freedom, duty, and truth

would be part of an integrated, harmonious whole
that were in balance with one another.

On the other hand, one could not be both stable
(a messianic trait) and unstable (a charismatic
property). Moreover, one cannot seek to genuinely
enhance the welfare of other people (a messianic
characteristic) and, at the same time, be antisocial
(a charismatic quality).

One cannot be both relatively humble (a
messianic tendency) and engaged in self-
aggrandizement (a charismatic inclination); nor
can one both sincerely seek to be removed from the
world's corruption (a messianic characteristic), as
well as exploit that corruption to justify one's own
descent into one's own amoral version of such
corruption (a charismatic quality). One cannot be
both attentive to the external world and, as a result,
be capable of monitoring one's behavior in the light
of that world (a messianic property), while,
simultaneously, being out of touch with that
external world and, therefore, unable to run
various kinds of reality checks intended to
constrain one's behavior (a charismatic property).

Furthermore, Oakes does not directly discuss
the possibility of there being 'prophets' who were
stable (messianic) but caught up in the throes of
self-aggrandizement (charismatic), or 'prophets'
who were interested in serving God (messianic)
but wanted recognition for their efforts
(charismatic). Oakes also does not speak about
'prophets' who might engage in reality checks

(messianic) and, yet, also have a tendency to rebel, flaunt convention, and become entangled with legal skirmishes of one kind or another (charismatic) ... in other words, a person might pay attention to the external world in order to better understand how to subvert it and manipulate it.

One could expand upon the nature and number of such permutations and combinations. Almost all, if not all, of the foregoing possibilities fall outside the horizons set by Oakes' exploration into the psychology of charisma.

One does not know how Oakes would respond to any of the foregoing possibilities other than, perhaps, to acknowledge them as issues that require further study. What one does know is that, in general, Oakes is inclined to place messianic prophets in a largely, if not wholly, spiritual-religious context, whereas so-called charismatic prophets tend to be perceived as individuals who do not necessarily participate in activities that can be described in religious, spiritual, or mystical terms.

Thus, individuals such as Hitler, Freud, Perls, and Erhard can be studied along side of overtly religious/spiritual figures such as Madame Blavatsky, Gurdjieff, Bhagwan Shree Rajneesh, Jim Jones, and Joseph Smith -- to name but a few. This is because the characteristic that ties these individuals together is not spirituality, per se, but the quality of charisma that can be manifested in both religious as well as nonreligious contexts.

One wonders why Oakes chose to use the term 'prophet' -- as opposed to, say, 'leader' or some other comparable word -- in order to refer to individuals who: proclaim a mission of salvation, seek to challenge or overthrow conventional values through that mission, and, in the process, try to induce people to participate in that mission by, among other things, applying the mission principles to their own lives through looking to the 'individual on a mission' as their guide or teacher concerning how one should go about accomplishing this. One possibility is that Oakes wanted to concentrate on what he perceived to be the 'function' of a 'prophet', independently of religious and spiritual considerations.

Thus, if one removes the element of spirituality from the idea of a prophet and just looks at the behavior of such an individual, then according to Oakes, prophets are individuals who: (a) proclaim a mission; (b) couch the nature of that mission in terms of some kind of salvation; (c) often run into conflict with certain conventional values that exist at the time the mission is pursued; (d) seek to attract adherents to the mission, and (e) serve as a guide or teacher for those individuals who are trying to incorporate the mission's principles into their lives. If one separates the element of spirituality and religiosity from the 'functional behavior' of a prophet, then individuals -- irrespective of whether they represented a religious or non-religious context -- might be considered to be observing 'prophetic' behavior if they satisfied the five conditions specified by Oakes that have been outlined above.

From a traditional, spiritual perspective, an individual does not proclaim himself or herself to be a 'prophet' or become a prophet by arbitrarily proclaiming that one has a mission. A Prophet is someone who is said to have been appointed by Divinity to serve in a particular capacity for a given community.

Secondly, to reduce the task of a Prophet down to being a mission of salvation is problematic. To be sure, prophets do speak about the issue of salvation, but they also speak about: knowledge, truth, spiritual potential, identity, purpose, justice, death, and purity in ways that transcend mere salvation and re-orients one toward the possibility of additional realms of the sacred—sometimes referred to as the mystical dimension of spirituality.

Thirdly, to say that the intention of a Prophet is to clash with conventional values, or to rebel against such values, or to start a revolutionary movement that opposes such values, this also is problematic. A Prophet of God seeks to speak and behave in accordance with the truth -- the reality of things -- and while it might be the case that what is true does conflict with certain, conventional values, the purpose of giving voice to the truth is not necessarily to generate conflict, rebellion, or revolution.

Moreover, even if it were true that some conventional values were opposed by a given Prophet, one need not suppose that, therefore, all conventional values in a certain community would become the focus of opposition. Whether conventional values became objects of conflict, or which values might became objects of conflict, could depend on a variety of circumstances and, consequently, to maintain that a main feature of the 'prophetic' mission is to revolutionize conventional values is far too sweeping and ambiguous a claim.

Prophets -- in a traditional spiritual sense -- are sent to remind and warn people about a variety of things. They are sent to induce people to seek out the truth in all things. They are appointed in order to encourage people to be loving, thankful, sincere, honest, kind, forgiving, tolerant, modest, generous, considerate, friendly, respectful, aware, co-operative, hopeful, persevering, patient, peaceful, and to be inclined toward seeking repentance (with respect to both human beings and God) for the mistakes one might have made. Prophets also are sent to discourage people from being: deceitful, exploitive, abusive, unjust, lacking in compassion, cruel, arrogant, hypocritical, dogmatic, intolerant, unloving, unfriendly, disputatious, immodest, thoughtless, insensitive, and so on.

There might be vested interests and various centers of power who become threatened, for one reason or another, by the activity of a Prophet, but the intent of a Prophet is not necessarily to wage war or rebel against those who have vested interests. Historically speaking, whenever and wherever possible, conciliation, harmony, peace, compromise, and negotiation are pursued by Prophets ... not confrontation and conflict.

Fourthly, a Prophet is not necessarily trying to attract followers. A Prophet is seeking to speak the truth as well as to offer guidance for anyone who is willing to engage that truth and guidance with a receptive heart and mind.

A Prophet is trying to assist people to realize the potential of their own relationship with the Truth/Reality. The fact that a community of people might arise around that individual might only mean that they are a community with a common set of purposes rather than an amalgamation made up of a leader and his or her followers.

Of course, the foregoing points all raise the question of whether, or not, there is anyone who is actually appointed by Divinity to serve in a special, Divinely-ordained role of a Prophet. For the most part, Oakes tries to stay away from this issue and, therefore, restricts his discussion to what people claim to believe concerning their status as a 'prophet', quite independently of considerations concerning the truth or falsity of those claims.

However, Oakes does stray from a largely neutral stance when he says that messianic prophets tend to operate in accordance with the 'fantasy' that they are -- in a yet to be explained (and possibly ineffable) sense -- "part" of God, whereas charismatic prophets are, according to Oakes, motivated by the 'fantasy' that they and the Godhead (or the psychic mother/father) are one ... that they are 'God'. In other words, Oakes is making a statement about what he perceives to be the truth status of much of what a 'prophet' says when Oakes maintains that no matter whether one falls into the category of a messianic prophet or one is subsumed under the category of a charismatic prophet, both sets of individuals are motivated by a fantasy concerning their relationship with God.

One is free to believe whatever she or he likes about the truth or falsity concerning the existence of Divinity, or the 'authenticity' of a given spiritual claim about being a 'Prophet'. However, one cannot claim to have an aura of neutrality on such issues, while simultaneously trying to claim that, say, someone's understanding concerning the nature of his or her relationship with Divinity is necessarily rooted in fantasies of one kind or another.

To be sure, there are individuals who do suffer from delusions concerning their self-professed Divine nature or special status with God, and so on. Nevertheless, this does not automatically force one to conclude that anyone who makes such statements is delusional or under the influence of a fantasy or myth of some kind. This remains to be determined on a case-by-case basis ... to the extent that it can be determined at all in any conclusive manner.

One cannot assume one's conclusions. Assumptions ought to be clearly identified as such, and there should be some thought given to how one's conclusions might be affected, adversely or otherwise, if the operational definition one is using -- in this case, the idea of who and what a 'prophet is -- turns out to be problematic, skewed, or incorrect.

Further evidence of the foregoing bias shows up in a variety of places in Oakes' book, but, perhaps, one of the clearest expressions of this slant comes in the conclusion when Oakes asks, and then answers, a question:

"But is the prophet really an enlightened spiritual being? If this question asks whether the prophet has personally experienced with the fullness of his being -- with his feelings and his relationships -- a spiritual reality, then, the answer appears to be no. Indeed, quite the opposite is true; it is the very shallowness of the prophet's feelings and relationships, his pervasive narcissism that prevents him from ever entering into a genuine relationship with another, or ever having anything other than pseudo feelings for others."

The foregoing statements might be quite accurate in their portrayal of the individuals whom Oakes actually studied in the field, and, as well, this sort of characterization might even be true of many of the religious, revolutionary, and charismatic personalities about whom Oakes learned during that phase of his research. In addition, Oakes is making an important point when he makes the quality of behavior a crucial, defining feature in determining whether, or not, someone should be considered to be a fully realized spiritual being.

Nonetheless, one hesitates to apply Oakes' conclusions across the board to any and all 'prophets'. Although he does not say so directly, the implication of his foregoing perspective tends to extend to such spiritual luminaries as: Jesus, Moses, Muhammad, the Buddha, Krishna, David, Solomon, Joseph, Abraham, and a host of others who, collectively, are considered by billions of people to be emissaries and prophets of Divinity.

To be sure, in the context of Oakes' study, the aforementioned remarks concerning whether, or not, prophets are spiritually realized human beings is primarily intended to refer to those individuals who fall into the category of 'charismatic prophet'. However, and as will be developed shortly, because Oakes' idea of charisma is, itself, problematic, a variety of difficulties arise in conjunction with his belief that, in general, 'prophets' are not really enlightened spiritual beings.

Part of the problem here is that some of the previously noted characteristics that, supposedly, differentiate between messianic and charismatic prophets raise some questions. For example, Oakes claims that one of the distinguishing features of a charismatic prophet is that such individuals tend to identify themselves with the Godhead, and, so, one might be puzzled about the idea of prophets not being spiritually realized human beings when one remembers that Jesus (peace be upon him) is reported to have said: "I and my Father are one" (this is a statement of unity, not necessarily identity or incarnation).

Is Oakes prepared to claim that Jesus (peace be upon him) was not only an unrealized spiritual being but, as well, was, if one accepts Oakes' logic, a charismatic prophet who was narcissistic and incapable of forming genuine, sincere, loving relationships with other human beings? If so, where is the evidence for this, and, if not, then perhaps, his theoretical framework will have to be modified accordingly.

Or, consider another possibility. According to Oakes, two of the characteristics of a charismatic prophet involve (a) locating Divinity within, rather than through external channels, and (b) filtering one's relationship with 'being' through a set of impersonal forces rather than through a personal relationship with a 'God'.

Presumably, on the basis of the foregoing, one might be required to place 'the Buddha' in the category of a 'charismatic prophet' since Buddhism is often portrayed, rightly or wrongly, as filtering one's relationship with Being through non-theistic forces of, to some extent, an impersonal nature. Yet, if one does this, is one forced to conclude that 'the Buddha' was a spiritually unrealized human being who was inclined to narcissism and only capable of having pseudo, shallow relationships with other individuals?

Similar questions arise in conjunction with some of the remarks made by Oakes concerning the Prophet Muhammad. For example, Oakes indicates (page 182) that Muhammad was among a group of historical personalities who led successful movements and passed away with their integrity intact-- i.e., no scandals. Oakes also identifies others who he judges to be like the Prophet Muhammad in this regard – e.g., Father Divine, Phineas Quimby, Prabhupada, Kathryn Kuhlman, and Ann Lee -- that is, 'prophets' who led successful, scandal-free movements.

These are individuals who did not self-destruct as is the tendency of many individuals who might fall into the category of 'charismatic prophets. Yet, at another juncture in his book (page 94), Oakes seeks to use Muhammad as an example of a historical prophet who, in Oakes' opinion, "played the part of a wounded innocent", by going into seclusion, in order to manipulate his wives into accepting his "dalliance with a slave girl".

Oakes does not provide any evidence to support his interpretation of the foregoing judgment. He states the foregoing as if it were an obvious fact and beyond question.

However, why should one accept such a judgment or interpretation? Why should one suppose that Muhammad was 'playing' the role of a 'wounded innocent'? Why should one suppose that he was trying to manipulate anyone? Why should one suppose that his relationship with the 'slave girl' was a mere "dalliance"?

Oakes is using a number of pejorative labels in reference to this prophet. Where is the independent evidence which indicates that any of his ways of describing the situation are evidentially warranted rather than expressions of Oakes' arbitrary biases being imposed on something about which he has no genuine insight or understanding?

For Oakes, one of the defining features of charismatic prophets is their capacity for, and willingness to, manipulate others. Indeed, one of the features that, supposedly, permits us to differentiate 'messianic prophets' from 'charismatic prophets' is the amazing social insight possessed by members of the latter category -- a capacity that, according to Oakes, allows such individuals to, in a sense, know which buttons to push in order to maneuver people in a desired direction.

Consequently, as was the case with respect to the implications of Oakes' foregoing quote -- for both Jesus and the Buddha -- concerning the lack of spiritual enlightenment in relation to 'prophets', once again, one is faced with an implication that paints Muhammad as someone who, according to the implications of Oakes' logic, might have been spiritually unenlightened, narcissistic, manipulative, and capable of only superficial, shallow relationships with others.

One of the arguments that some individuals have leveled against theoreticians like Freud is that he used his understanding of abnormal behavior and psycho-pathology to set the tone for what he considered to be healthy, normal psychological development. According to such critics, when one starts with a certain kind of sample set -- namely, people suffering from pathology -- one might not be able to validly make the transition from: what that sample says about the nature of the people in such a sample, to: claims concerning the psychology of human nature in a population of people who do not suffer from such pathology.

Similarly, by using certain, arbitrarily decided-upon, behavioral and functional characteristics of individuals as the basis for labeling various individuals as 'prophets', one might wish to pause for a moment and ask whether the behavioral and functional characteristics being cited really are reflective of how an actual 'Prophet' might think, feel, act, or be motivated. Even if one wishes to argue that the latter considerations should not shape and orient a study in psychology, nevertheless, one still needs to take note of the lacunae that are, potentially, present when a researcher tries to do an end-around, or ignore, the idea of 'authenticity' with respect to someone who claims to be, or is perceived to be, a prophet in a traditional sense, and, as a result, employs arbitrarily chosen criteria to shape the operational definitions one uses to establish categories, differentiate individuals, and orient one's research.

If the definition of a 'prophet' does not necessarily reflect historical and/or traditional considerations, and if the sample being studied does not necessarily reflect historical and/or traditional 'realities' concerning the lives of Prophets, then at the very least, one should raise a caveat concerning the validity of applying the results of a given study -- like that of Oakes -- to a larger population containing some individuals who might actually be individuals who were appointed by Divinity to pursue goals, purposes, and activities that are in contradistinction to Oakes's operational definition of 'prophet' and who are neither necessarily delusional nor under the influence of one, or another, fantasy with respect to their relationship with Divinity.

What difference do the foregoing considerations make with respect to understanding the idea of 'prophetic charisma' or the psychology of revolutionary, religious personalities? As it turns out, perhaps a great many problematic ramifications might arise as a result of such considerations, and this might be most clearly described and explained through an examination of the way in which Oakes talks about two other themes -- charisma and narcissism -- within the context of a theory that claims to be directed toward helping us understand the nature of: 'prophetic charisma'.

I do not feel it would be distorting Oakes' position to say that, to a major extent, the phenomenon of charisma is, for him, an expression of, and rooted in, the phenomenon of narcissism. At least, this does seem to be the case as far as the idea of the psychology of religious personalities is concerned -- both with respect to 'prophets' as well as their followers.

Oakes indicates that someone can be referred to as charismatic when she or he is perceived to embody something referred to as "ultimate concerns". While this embodiment of ultimate concerns might be in relation to either oneself or others, however, the meaning of 'ultimate concern' tends to vary from person to person.

Nonetheless, when an individual has extraordinary needs in relation to whatever a given 'ultimate concern' might turn out to be for that person (and extraordinary needs are linked to the formation of a nuclear-self early in life that is colored by, among other things, narcissistic forces), then according to Oakes, the perception of the embodiment of that ultimate concern in another human being gives expression to an extremely powerful magnetic force of attraction. This conjunction of 'ultimate concerns', 'extraordinary needs', and the 'embodiment' of such concerns in a person who, as a result, is perceived to be a vehicle for: accessing, being in proximity to, and/or realizing such ultimate concerns, is considered, by Oakes, to beat the heart of the phenomenon of charisma.

Although the foregoing description does not specifically limit charisma to spiritual contexts, nonetheless, Oakes does believe that charisma constitutes a spiritual power with a considerable potential to revolutionize society. Moreover, he believes charisma has the capacity to spiritualize the extraordinary needs and ultimate concerns of those who are seeking to have their needs and concerns fulfilled.

It is hard, at this point, to understand just what Oakes means by the idea that charisma can spiritualize ultimate concerns and extraordinary needs. If a given ultimate concern is not already spiritual in nature, or if an extraordinary need is not already rooted in spirituality of one kind or another, then how does charisma, per se, spiritualize either ultimate concerns or extraordinary needs? What does it mean to spiritualize something?

Furthermore, since Oakes has indicated that charisma is a function of the perception that someone embodies the ultimate concerns of oneself or others, and since Oakes has indicated that charisma is a function of the perception that someone will serve as a means to the fulfillment of one's extraordinary needs, then one wonders about the precise dynamics of how either charisma, or its alleged spiritualizing dimension, works. After all, on the basis of the foregoing considerations, charisma seems to be something that is conferred on a given human being -- e.g., a 'prophet' -- as a result of the perceived embodiment of one's ultimate concerns in, say, a 'prophet' due to the extraordinary needs of the one doing the perceiving.

If the foregoing characterization of things is correct, then charisma is not something that a 'prophet' possesses. Rather, charisma arises -- and, sometimes, Oakes appears to suggest as much -- when the right alignment of 'prophet', 'ultimate concerns', 'extraordinary needs', and perception takes place. As such, charisma is a function of the dynamics of a certain kind of relationship between two, or more, people.

What a seeker brings to the equation are: ultimate concerns, extraordinary needs, and a perceptual mind-set that is actively or passively looking for something that resonates with those concerns and needs. What a 'prophet' brings to this dynamic are his or her own kind of extraordinary needs, together with a set of qualities that not only resonate, to some degree, with the concerns and needs of the seeker, but which, as well, are perceived to have something of a supernatural-like aura about them.. that is, there is something about the relationship that appears to be largely inexplicable, magical, mysterious, and resistant to any kind of easy explanation ... something that is experienced as seductive, alluring, magnetic, compelling, and somewhat mesmerizing.

One of the qualities that Oakes believes plays a significant role in the felt presence of charisma is the 'prophet's' talent for observation and an accompanying special ability to derive, from such observations, penetrating insights into the nature of on-going social dynamics as well as the extraordinary needs and ultimate concerns of individuals who engage the 'prophet'. Someone once remarked that one society's technology might appear like magic to another society that does not understand the principles through which such technology operates, and, similarly, when someone does not understand how a given person has arrived at her or his insight into one's extraordinary needs, ultimate concerns, or the surrounding social dynamics, then the individual with insight might be perceived as someone who has magical-like, supernatural-like capabilities and powers simply because one might not understand how such insight is possible.

Do some 'prophets' actually have psychic, occult, extrasensory, or non-ordinary powers of perception? Oakes does not believe so.

He believes everything is explicable through the manner in which ordinary abilities and talents might be developed to an amazing degree by individuals who have extraordinary needs. These needs are dependent for their fulfillment on the existence and use of such capabilities.

Oakes maintains (page 188) that a charismatic relationship begins with a seeker's surrender and trust. According to Oakes, only later does the seeker begin to project her or his own ultimate concerns onto the 'prophet' and through this projection become 'fused' with the person of the 'prophet' to such a degree that the 'seeker' interacts with the 'prophet' as if the latter individual were an expression of one's own inner, deeper, more essential 'self'.

If so, this leaves unanswered the question of why someone would trust or surrender to another individual without some sort of substantial motivation for doing so? Apparently, Oakes seems to be saying that trust and surrender arise prior to, and independently of, the establishing of a charismatic relationship that, according to Oakes, revolves around the dynamics of 'extraordinary needs', 'ultimate concerns', and the perceived embodiment of these qualities in the person of the 'prophet' -- something that Oakes claims happens later in the relationship and, therefore, does not appear to be the initial reason why someone trusts and surrenders to the 'prophet'.

According to Oakes, charisma spiritualizes a relationship. Yet, somehow, trust and surrender -- which, presumably, are essential to any sort of spiritual relationship -- take place, on Oakes' account, before the main component of a charismatic relationship -- namely, the perceived presence of the embodiment of ultimate concerns -- is established.

The foregoing sequence of events appears somewhat counterintuitive. A more likely explanation would seem to involve the possibility that the felt or perceived presence of charisma is what helps induce someone to trust and surrender to a 'prophet', and, if this is the case, then Oakes might be mistaken about when the projection of ultimate concerns on to a 'prophet' takes place.

Furthermore, one wonders if it is so much a matter of a 'seeker's' projection of ultimate concerns onto the 'prophet', as it might be a matter of such ultimate concerns actually being reflected in, or resonating with, some, or all, of the words and behaviors of the 'prophet'. In other words, is one to suppose that the perception of the embodiment of ultimate concerns in another human being is merely a delusion in which nothing of those ultimate concerns actually is present in what a 'prophet' says and does, or should one assume that, to varying degrees, something of a substantive nature concerning such ultimate concerns is actually touched upon by the teachings and actions of the 'prophet'?

To be sure, a seeker could be mistaken. For example, a seeker might believe that something of his or her ultimate concerns was present in what the 'prophet's said and did, only to discover, subsequently, that such was not the case or that whatever was present was being expressed in a fraudulent and manipulative manner. Or, a seeker initially might believe that a given 'prophet' could serve as a venue through which the seeker's extraordinary needs and ultimate concerns could be realized, only to, later on, come to the conclusion, rightly or wrongly, that the 'prophet' could not actually assist one to fulfill one's extraordinary needs or ultimate concerns. Alternatively, a seeker's first, cursory impression of a 'prophet' might have led the seeker to believe that the prophet and the seeker shared a set of common concerns, values, and the like, only to realize, upon closer inspection, that the two, despite initial impressions, really weren't on the same page with respect to a variety of issues, concerns, goals, and values.

However, such mistakes are not necessarily delusional in character. They are beliefs that come to be, hopefully, constructively modified in the light of subsequent experience -- something (that is, constructive modification) to which delusions are inherently resistant.

As such, it is not ultimate concerns, per se, that are being projected onto the prophet/leader/teacher. Instead, what is being projected is a hope concerning the potential value of what might ensue in relation to one's ultimate concerns by linking up with someone claiming to be a prophet/guide/leader.

Trust and surrender are offered in exchange for a promissory note, of sorts, about future considerations in conjunction with the fulfillment of extraordinary needs and ultimate concerns. The felt presence of charisma is perceived, rightly or wrongly, as an indicator that someone -- namely, a prophet/leader/teacher -- can satisfy the conditions of that promissory note. The felt presence of charisma, justifiably or unjustifiably, tends to create certain kinds of expectations concerning the fulfillment of ultimate concerns and extraordinary needs in the future.

Notwithstanding the foregoing considerations, one still is unclear about what charisma is or how the perceived presence of charisma has the capacity to induce or inspire trust, surrender, and expectations concerning one's ultimate concerns and extraordinary needs. One has a sense that, somehow, the perceived presence of charisma might have a 'spiritualizing effect in as much as trust and surrender -- which are important components of spirituality -- might be engendered, somehow, through the presence of something called 'charisma', and, yet, the manner in which this takes place -- the dynamics of the spiritualizing process -- remains elusive and puzzling.

Oakes believes that the secret of charisma lies in a narcissistic dimension of human development. More specifically, he believes that the alleged 'extraordinary needs' of both a 'prophet' and a seeker are entangled in the agenda of a 'nuclear self' which forms under certain conditions that, according to Oakes, are conducive to the emergence of narcissistic personality disorder in, at the very least, 'a charismatic prophet'.

Although at one point in his discussion of the phenomenon of narcissistic development Oakes voices a cautionary note concerning the question of how well can we know the mind and inner life of another human being, nevertheless, he soon leaves such caution behind when delineating Kohut's theory of narcissism and seeks to link that theory to the idea of charisma. Of course, generally speaking, it is often part and parcel of theoretical work to take some risks while venturing into uncharted conceptual territory, but some risks might be more viable than others.

Heinz Kohut developed his theory of narcissism while treating patients with narcissistic personality disorder. Based upon his experiences with such patients, he sought to explain the origins of that disorder.

The patients being treated by Kohut tended to possess a grandiose sense of self-confidence, untouched by any sort of self-doubt. They often were very perceptive about people and social dynamics (sometimes uncannily so), could be quite persuasive, but also were given to blaming and accusing others of various failings and short-comings.

Such patients frequently were inclined toward exhibitionism and were given to voicing unrealistic, naïve fantasies concerning themselves and their place in the scheme of things. In addition, these individuals tended to demonstrate little evidence of possessing a conscience or experiencing any sort of guilt when involved in wrong doing. Moreover, their relationships with others usually were marked by an almost complete absence of empathy for people and, as well, appeared to be imbued with a belief that other people existed to serve the needs of the narcissist.

According to Freud, all of us go through a period of primary narcissism during infancy when we believe that everything not only revolves around us but that the world is, in a sense, a creation of our own. Furthermore, this period of narcissism is said to be characterized by a child's sense of oneness with the world (meaning the mothering-one) that is posited to be a continuation of one's life in the womb when, supposedly, the boundaries between mother and child are completely dissolved.

During this period of felt-oneness, the child is said to bask in the nurturing glow of exaltation transmitted through the mother's gaze and treatment of the child. Through this sort of adoring interaction, the child feels worshiped and develops a sense of uninhibited, grandiose omnipotence that permeates the mind-set of the infant.

In the course of normal development, Freud indicates that primary narcissism becomes significantly attenuated and modulated as experience introduces a child to the pain of feeling alone in a world that, in many ways, appears indifferent to the desires of the child. Feelings of omnipotence are ravaged by the onslaught of a sense of helplessness.

With the waning of primary narcissism, a child no longer believes herself or himself to be the center of the universe. A Copernican–like revolution has shaken the foundations of the child's previously Ptolemaic existence.

The idea of 'primary narcissism' is a theoretical construct. Whether a fetus or an infant ever has a sense of oneness with the mother, or whether an infant ever operates out of a framework that is permeated with feelings of omnipotence and grandiosity, or whether an infant ever operates under the illusion/delusion that she or he is the creative and causal force behind the happenings of the universe, or whether an infant ever has a sense of being worshiped like a 'god', or whether an infant ever has the sense that he or she shares a state of perfection with a 'saintly' mothering one -- all of these are highly contentious, largely speculative considerations.

Instead, one might entertain the possibility that any deeply developed notion of primary narcissism in the Freudian sense might have a very difficult time becoming established amidst the realities of this world. After all, almost from the first spank on the bottom that introduces us to this plane of existence, there is a great deal of human experience indicating: that we are not omnipotent; that however intimate one's relationship with the mothering-one might be, there is felt separation in the sense that there are very real differences between how the mothering-one behaves and how we might wish the mothering-one to behave; that we cannot always make the nipple appear upon demand; that the discomfort of wet diapers or a colic-ridden system does not always disappear with the mere wish for this to be so; that we are not in control of how hot or cold we feel; that the ravages of colds, fevers and illness descend upon us without our permission; that an infant might have difficulty in believing that she or he rules over the universe when he or she can't even get her or his hands and fingers to go where he or she would like or accomplish what she or he would like with such appendages.

The bundle of problematic desires, wishes, impulses, thoughts, and motivations within each of us that collectively are subsumed under the term "id" is a very different entity than the idea of primary narcissism. There is a considerable amount of metaphysical theory (e.g., oneness, omnipotence, and grandiosity, being worshiped, shared state of perfection), infusing the concept of primary narcissism that is absent from the notion of 'id' that simply posits, based on observation and experience, that there are wishes, desires, thoughts, and motivations within us seeking expression and that tend to generate a sense of frustration or anger when the sought-for realizations are blocked, thwarted, or ignored in various ways.

Leaving aside such considerations for the moment, let's return to Kohut's theory of narcissism. According to Kohut, the mothering-one filters the tendency of the world to intrude into the life of an infant, and, as a result, the mothering one has a role to play in helping to gradually initiate an infant into the realities of the world and away from the influence of the condition of primary narcissism.

Sometimes, however, Kohut maintains that something happens and the filtering process breaks down. There is some sort of traumatic tear in the process and, in one way or another, the child is deprived not only of the filtering assistance afforded by the mothering-one but, as well, the child loses the process of gradual initiation into the realities of the world ... realties that undermine and attack the child's sense of primary narcissism.

As a result, Kohut believes that some children, when faced with such a traumatic situation, seek to assume the responsibility of managing the filtering/initiation process by using the condition of primary narcissism as a coping strategy to try to filter and fend off the demands of the world. In such individuals, rather than the condition of primary narcissism becoming attenuated and modulated over time, this condition becomes strengthened and comes to dominate many aspects of that person's way of interacting with the world.

Although those individuals who become inclined to filter reality through the colored lenses of primary narcissism do learn -- through trial and error (sometimes with great difficulty) -- how the world operates and how to negotiate many different kinds of problematic encounters with the world in a way that will help to avoid punishment while garnering various rewards, nonetheless, Kohut believes that, for the most part, such people are ensconced in a paradigm of reality that is: self-serving, largely (if not completely) devoid of empathy for others, lacking in conscience, steeped in a sense of grandiosity concerning oneself, constantly seeking feedback from others that validates that sense of grandiosity, and are often skilled in insightful social observation as well as the art of persuading and/or manipulating others to become tools for the acquisition of whatever is desired or sought ... especially positive feedback concerning one's fantasies and delusions about grandiosity (this is often referred to as 'narcissistic supply').

Anyone who opposes, seeks to constrain, or interferes with the paradigm of primary narcissism through which the world is perceived and engaged by someone in the throes of narcissistic personality disorder is likely to become the focal object of what Kohut refers to as 'narcissistic rage'. Such interlopers are resented, resisted, and riled against -- either openly and/or through various forms of indirect stratagems in which people become pawns to be used, and if necessary sacrificed, to check the perceived antagonist.

Kohut distinguishes between messianic personalities and charismatic personalities (rather than 'leaders' or prophets') within the foregoing context of primary narcissism gone awry. The messianic personality is someone who projects a sense of grandiosity outward in the form of an 'object' and identifies this externalized, "idealized superego", or 'self', as a 'god' who is to be served, worshiped and from whom revelation/guidance is received. The charismatic personality, on the other hand, is someone who internalizes the sense of grandiosity and equates one's own being with an idealized sense of the omnipotent 'self' or Godhead that is to serve as an example for others.

Kohut believes a messianic personality is pulled by externalized ideals and the challenge of trying to emulate and live up to those ideals. A charismatic personality, however, is driven by ambitions revolving about her or his need for self-aggrandizement, together with a validation of that sense of grandiosity through the recognition and acknowledgment of others.

Following up on an idea of Kohut's, Oakes advances the theoretical possibility that 'seekers' might hook up with 'prophets' in ways that are mutually accommodating. In other words, individuals who have had their own problems negotiating the transition from primary narcissism to a more 'realistic' way of understanding that the world does not revolve around one's existence, might have 'extraordinary needs' that a messianic or charismatic prophet is perceived to be able to address and/or resolve. By helping a messianic or charismatic prophet to validate his or her sense of reality through the act of following such an individual, a seeker hopes to receive, in return, what might be needed in the way of the satisfaction of the seeker's ultimate concerns that will permit that individual to be happy, transformed, content, at peace, in harmony with one self or the world, or whatever else might be the thrust of the ultimate concerns and 'extraordinary needs' of a psychological/emotional nature inherent in the seeker.

Presumably, those individuals who identified with, or felt resonance in, the coping strategy adopted by a messianic personality, prophet or leader, would gravitate toward, or be attracted by, or feel 'at home' in circumstances where the 'idealized superego' had been projected outward and could be sought in the external world as an 'object' of some kind through which one's world could be ordered, guided, and ethically oriented. On the other hand, those individuals who identified or found resonance with the coping strategy developed by a charismatic personality, prophet or leader, might be inclined toward, attracted by, or feel comfortable in an environment where the 'grandiose self' was sought within and, if located, could lead to a sense of omnipotence, freedom, and primal release.

Although there is a certain degree of coherence and consistency to the foregoing theoretical framework and without wishing to argue that there is no one (either among 'prophets' or followers) who operates in accordance with such psychological dynamics, nonetheless, there are a great many reservations one might have concerning such a theory. For instance, to assume that all people externalize an 'idealized superego' or identify with an internalized 'grandiose self' might be a way of accounting for the observed behavior of some individuals, but such an assumption also tends to prevent one from considering the possibility that truth and reality are not necessarily a function of what we project, create, or identify with but might exist quite independently of what we think, feel, and believe.

Not every search for the truth is necessarily a reflection of unresolved issues of primary narcissism. Not every issue of ethics or morality necessarily reduces down to what we seek to impose on reality or what we internalize in the way of parental values. Not every search for identity is necessarily a function of the nuclear self's agenda that, according to Kohut and Oakes, precipitates out of the transition from primary narcissism to more mature modes of interaction. Not every search for wisdom is necessarily a reflection of the development of coping strategies for psychic survival. Not every search for justice is necessarily a reflection of one's likes and dislikes. Not every search for guidance is necessarily an exercise in finding a match between a 'prophet's' psychological profile and one's own psychological needs.

Not every 'prophet' is necessarily a product of the psychodynamics of everyday life. Not every thought of awe or omnipotence is necessarily either self-referential or a matter of what one projects onto the universe. Not every experience of love is necessarily a mirrored reflection of the presence of narcissism. Not all dissatisfactions concerning the limitations, problems, and lacuna of psychoanalytical thought are necessarily evidence that denial and other defense mechanisms are at work to save us from the painful realization of repressed wishes, fantasies, impulses, and thoughts.

What is the truth concerning such matters? Whatever they might be, one shouldn't start out by, in various ways, pre-judging the matter.

One cannot claim to be objective while being predisposed to restrict one's investigation to purely psychological principles in relation to some phenomenon without examining the possible merits of metaphysical or trans-personal explanations with respect to that same issue. One cannot claim to be value-neutral while ignoring possible data, experience, and phenomena that are not necessarily consistent with one's philosophical and/or psychological orientation.

Oakes admits that trying to trace such ideas as messianic and charismatic personalities back to the dynamics of infantile phenomenology is a speculative exercise (e.g., page 42). However, at other times he speaks in terms that appear to transpose these speculative exercises into 'likely' explanations of this or that phenomenon, or this or that individual (and, I have already pointed out that almost none of what Oakes or Kohut have to say is 'likely' to be accurately reflective of the lives, teachings and personalities of such individuals as Jesus, the Buddha, or Muhammad, not to mention any number of other spiritual luminaries who appear among the ranks of both historical Prophets and the great mystical guides from many different spiritual traditions).

Although it is desirable to want to subsume as large a body of phenomena, behavior, and data, as is possible, under the rubric of one theoretical framework, one also has to be prepared to acknowledge the possibility that reality might be far more complex, rich, nuanced, and problematic than the capabilities of any single theory. Moreover, while certain individuals might exhibit behavior and characteristics that are compatible with, say, the theories of Kohut, nevertheless, this does not automatically preclude the possibility that there might be many individuals who do not demonstrate profiles that easily, if at all, conform to the requirements of such a theory. Indeed, there might be a variety of different currents of human potential that are running through the ocean we call 'reality'.

One might be willing to accept Kohut's psychoanalytical theory concerning the way in which some individuals supposedly deal with the problem of primary narcissism. Nonetheless, even if one were to accept

Kohut's tendency to conceive of the difference between messianic personalities and charismatic personalities as being a function of whether, respectively, an 'idealized superego' was externalized or a 'grandiose self' was internalized, one still has difficulty understanding precisely how the ideas of 'prophet', 'narcissism', and charisma fit together.

Oakes does suggest that 'seekers' tend to be attracted to, or inclined toward, those 'leaders', 'guides', and 'prophets' who best reflect the 'extraordinary needs' of such 'seekers. As a result, some people are attracted to, and follow, messianic 'prophets', while others are attracted to, and follow, 'charismatic prophets'.

However, right away there is a problem here. If charisma is, to some extent, a function of the resonance of psychological profiles between, on the one hand, a 'prophet' or 'leader', and, on the other hand, a follower, then why refer to only one of the two classes of 'prophets' or 'teachers' as charismatic?

In both cases, there might be some sort of attraction involved. Yet, apparently, the attraction experienced in the case of so-called 'messianic prophets' is not an expression of charisma.

Of course, Oakes argues, quite explicitly, that charisma is very much rooted in someone -- 'prophet', 'teacher' 'leader' 'guide' -- being perceived to be the embodiment of another individual's ultimate concerns. Nonetheless, the same kind of question that was raised in the foregoing comments needs to be asked again.

More specifically, if one assumes, as seems logical to do, that both 'messianic prophets' and 'charismatic prophets' might be perceived to embody someone's ultimate concerns, then why does the adjective, charismatic only refer to one of the two classes of 'prophets'? Someone might counter, in Oakes's defense, by saying something along the lines of: 'Well, there are 'extraordinary needs' present in the case of the followers of 'charismatic prophets' that are not present among the followers of 'messianic prophets' and this phenomenon of 'extraordinary needs' together with the idea of the embodiment of ultimate concerns is what gives rise to the experience of charisma'.

However, such a possible response seems rather weak and not without its own problems. For example, if 'extraordinary needs' are a reflection of the unresolved issues of someone's psychological profile with respect to, say, primary narcissism, then why should one suppose that the needs of someone who seeks out and follows a 'messianic prophet' are any less extraordinary than the needs of someone who seeks out and follows a 'charismatic prophet'?

For example, why should one suppose that developmental problems surrounding the issue of an externalized 'idealized superego' are any less extraordinary than the developmental problems swirling about the internalization of a 'grandiose self'? What are the criteria for determining what constitutes "extraordinary needs"?

Furthermore, there are also some questions that ought to be directed to the alleged link between charisma and the perceived embodiment of ultimate concerns. In other words, just because someone is seen to embody the ultimate concerns of another individual, why should one automatically assume that the former person will be considered to be charismatic?

Oakes indicates that the meaning of 'ultimate concerns' will vary with the 'seeker' or 'follower' being considered. Ultimate concerns could be of a political, economic, ecological, philosophical, sexual, social, and/or spiritual nature.

We might consider our children to be expressions of our ultimate concerns, but this doesn't necessarily make those children charismatic. We might treat our careers as an expression of our ultimate concern, but this doesn't make our boss charismatic. We might believe that a given political leader embodies our ultimate concerns concerning a variety of social, legal, and economic issues, but we might not necessarily view the leader as charismatic so much as we might evaluate the 'leader' in terms of competence or incompetence, or in terms of someone who is popular or unpopular. A defendant in a murder trial might see his or her defense attorney, the judge, and the jury to be embodiments of her or his ultimate concerns concerning freedom, but this fact does not necessarily cause the defendant to perceive those other individuals as charismatic. We might believe that doctors, school teachers, police officials, fire fighters, and university professors might embody some of our ultimate concerns, but we don't necessarily consider those individuals to be charismatic. The members of a congregation or parish might perceive their minister, rabbi, priest, or imam to embody the ultimate concerns of the congregation, but those members do not necessarily consider such 'leaders' to be charismatic -- although they might consider them to be knowledgeable, approachable, compassionate, interesting, moral, and committed.

Consequently, one need not feel compelled to automatically agree that charisma is a function of the perception that someone embodies our ultimate concerns. Nor is it necessarily the case that charisma is a function of 'extraordinary needs' per se.

According to Oakes, individuals follow a 'prophet', 'leader', 'guru', or 'guide' for a reason (page 126). They are looking for something and come to believe, rightly or wrongly, that such a 'prophet' might be able to provide what they are looking for, or they need something and, rightly or wrongly, they come to believe that the 'prophet', leader, or teacher might be the key to the fulfillment or satisfaction of that need.

Oakes cautions his readers that trying to fathom the deeper motivations that shape the decisions that people make with respect to whether, or not, to follow a 'prophet', 'teacher' or 'leader' is an exercise in speculation. Oakes goes on to indicate that when the people whom he interviewed were asked why they joined a group or decided to follow a 'prophet/leader/guide', quite frequently, those being interviewed responded in terms of wanting to realize some sort of ideal -- such as enlightenment, salvation, or some similar "great work" that involved a transformation of the 'self' – and, yet, when these same individuals were asked what joining a group had permitted them to accomplish or what leaving such a group would mean to them, Oakes said that very different kinds of responses were given.

When the purpose of the 'great work' of self-transformation is not realized, followers often speak in terms of other kinds of values. For instance, they might speak about the process of having been part of something in which they placed their trust and to which they surrendered and that yielded certain kinds of experiential dividends and life lessons other than total self-transformation.

Some of these individuals might have had many of their illusions, naïve and otherwise, dispelled as physical proximity exposed the feet of clay of this or that 'prophet/guide/leader'. Yet, these same individuals might, nonetheless, feel a sense of gratitude for what they have experienced

305

and learned in conjunction with that 'leader/prophet/teacher'. Other individuals speak in terms of the satisfaction derived through having been able to work hard and achieve or learn things that, prior to joining, they might not have thought possible or expected of themselves.

Oakes mentions four qualities that he claims form the core of a follower's attachment to a 'prophet/teacher/leader'. These qualities are: (1) faith (very vaguely and amorphously defined), (2) trust, (3) courage (in the sense of the courage that a 'prophet' gives to seekers in his or her role of someone who, allegedly, has attained salvation or self-realization, and, therefore, is a living exemplar, supposedly, of what is within the grasp of one and all) , and (4) projection (the placing of one's ultimate concerns onto the figure of the 'prophet/guide/leader').

A charismatic 'prophet/leader/guide' could strengthen faith, or induce trust, or inspire courage, or provide a reason for why one believes that such a 'prophet' actually does embody one's ultimate concerns, and, therefore, represents a worthy recipient of such projection. However, admitting this possibility doesn't really make charisma something that is caused by some combination of faith, trust, courage, and/or projection, as much as this might indicate that charisma could play a causal role in the explanation of why someone becomes attached to a given 'prophet/leader/teacher' through faith, trust, courage and projection.

Similar sorts of comments could be made in relation to Oakes' contention that, for example, 'love' and 'freedom' are characteristic of groups led by 'charismatic prophets', whereas 'truth' and 'ethics' are associated with 'messianic prophets'. To begin with, it is not obvious, in any prima facie manner, that someone who is perceived to be an extraordinarily loving human being would necessarily be any more charismatic than someone who is rigorously devoted to the truth, or that someone who is an extreme individualist will necessarily be perceived as being more charismatic than someone who is devoted to duty with respect to moral and ethical issues.

We might be attracted to all of these kinds of individuals. Yet, such attraction is not necessarily of a charismatic kind. We might be attracted for other reasons such as having respect for such people or wanting to emulate them or wanting to learn from them or feeling comfortable around these kinds of individual.

One is still left wondering why messianic 'prophets/teachers/guides' aren't referred to as 'charismatic'. One also is still wondering why so-called 'charismatic prophets' are considered to be 'charismatic'.

Oakes devotes a whole chapter to the idea of the 'charismatic moment'. This is described as an instant, or relatively brief interval of time, in which a person is willing to open up one's heart, to lay bare one's soul, to trust without reservation, to become totally vulnerable to another and surrender.

The charismatic moment is to experience an exhilarating, intoxicating, powerful, intense, electric blurring of boundaries between oneself and the 'prophet/teacher/guide' and/or the group that is led by such an individual. These moments are said to give expression to a primal, life impulse (which Weber refers to as 'pure charisma') that might be charged with sexual energy and are often steeped in a shroud of mystery, secrecy, tension, the unpredictable, a leap into the unknown, and an exhilarating, edgy sort of riskiness -- all of which might intensify one's willingness to throw caution to the wind, abandon normal conventions, and become open to the moment.

According to Oakes' the 'charismatic prophet' is someone who is accomplished in inducing such moments through, among other means, establishing rituals conducive to the generation of charismatic moments. Oakes believes that such rituals are one of the most creative accomplishments of a 'charismatic prophet'.

However, Oakes also indicates (page 148) there often is a dimension of the whole process that is beyond the capacity of the 'prophet/teacher/guide', the group, or a follower, to control. More specifically, no one knows, for sure, whether, on any given occasion, the 'spirit' (or whatever it is that is transpiring at a given instant) will flow and the gathering will be anointed with the presence of a charismatic moment.

Apparently, charismatic moments do not necessarily flow through the teacher to the other participants. 'Prophets/leaders/teachers' cannot always produce these moments on demand. Consequently, while 'prophets/teachers/guides' might, or might not be, necessary conditions for the advent of a 'charismatic moment', they are not always sufficient conditions for such phenomena.

When reading Oakes, one often is puzzled because he sometimes alternates among a variety of expressions that are not necessarily reducible to a single phenomenon. Sometimes he talks about charismatic prophets -- and, indeed, the title of his book is Prophetic Charisma -- as if they are the source of, or channel for, charisma.

However, sometimes he talks about how charisma is a product of the way followers project their ultimate concerns onto a given 'prophet/leader/guide'. On still other occasions he talks about how charismatic prophets are very adept in creating rituals that can lead to the experience of charismatic moments and, yet, whether, or not, the spirit moves on such occasion seems to depend on something beyond what the 'prophet/teacher/leader' brings to the table in the way of creative rituals.

Oakes states that: people who are narcissistic personalities are often perceived as individuals who project an image of unshakeable confidence and strength concerning their purpose, role, and mission in life. Oakes also describes such individuals as being perceived as courageous, even fearless, with respect to those who oppose her or him. Moreover, the capacity of many narcissists to exhibit an uncanny sensitivity to social and individual psychological dynamics lends them an aura of someone with supernatural powers. Finally, because narcissists have an inflated sense of their own self-importance, they also tend to be perceived as being positive and upbeat about life.

A narcissistic individual might appear strong and self-confident because she or he cannot admit the possibility that he or she might not be whom she or he takes himself or herself to be. Such an admission is an anathema to the narcissist.

A narcissistic personality might appear courageous and fearless because, in a very real sense, their psychic survival depends on being able to oppose anything that would cast doubts upon, or bring into question, or cast aspersions and ridicule upon, the narcissist's beliefs about who she or he is and what role such an individual plays in the scheme of things. When opponents seek to put them in a corner, they often respond with the ferocity of someone fighting for survival -- a courage and fearlessness that can be camouflaged to appear as being in defense of truth and justice when it is really self-serving.

Oakes describes the charismatic prophet as someone who utilizes some of the strengths of his or her narcissistic condition to attract, influence, and manipulate seekers and followers. When people encounter someone who seems to be strong, self-confident, purposeful, committed, positive, courageous, fearless, and insightful, such people might be induced to consider those individuals to be extraordinary personalities and quite different from most other individuals, and depending on how adept the narcissist is in camouflaging the true significance and meaning of such qualities (that is, as expressions of a pathological strategy for coping in life rather than any form of spiritual accomplishment or realization), a narcissistic personality might, on the surface, seem like someone who possesses the 'pure charisma' that is believed to mark the 'anointed ones' of destiny or Divinity.

Oakes points out how the career choices of many people who go on to assume the role of a 'prophet/leader/guide' often have a connection to activities in which communication tends to play a central role. For example, on page 88, Oakes lists such careers as: entertainers, sales people, teachers, clergy, and counselors (especially in conjunction with alternative heath) as having prominence in the backgrounds of many of the people in his research.

People who have the gift of gab, people who are adept in the arts of social influence, people who have experience with using language skills to shape the ideas, opinions, values, and desires of other people -- all of these individuals are specialists in framing reality to serve their purposes. This need not mean that all such individuals are pursuing malevolent or exploitive purposes, but, under the right circumstances, this could be the case.

Narcissists who enjoy strong skills of communication, persuasion, influence and the framing of reality tend to use such skills in manipulative, controlling, and destructive ways. However, if a narcissist can succeed in inducing people to believe that something other than what is actually going on is going on, then this could be an extremely powerful means of altering another person's sense of reality, identity, purpose, truth, meaning, right, and wrong.

Finally, if one adds to the foregoing set of qualities an element of what is referred to as love, the package could assume quite a powerful presence in the perception of a seeker. Only much later, if at all, will a seeker discover that such 'love' is really nothing more than a manipulative device devoid of all empathy and compassion for another and solely geared toward priming the pump of narcissistic supply that is the life blood of a narcissistic personality and which is sucked from other human beings like a vampire with an inexhaustible hunger for that which they do not have and that can only be provided by warm bodies and souls.

In the beginning, however, all of this is hidden from view. First, superficial impressions might dominate the perception of a seeker – to the benefit of the narcissist and to the detriment of the seeker.

Presumably, it is the foregoing package of perceived qualities that helps a narcissistic personality to appear, to some, as a charismatic figure and, thereby, enable a 'prophet/leader/guide' to arrange for 'charismatic moments' that induce vulnerability, trust, surrender, and even a sense of complete abandon in some seekers/followers. The creation of such moments is part of the repertoire of tricks and stratagems the narcissist has picked up over the years to help manage his or her world in a way that permits a continuation in the flow of narcissistic supply to come to her or his way as followers -- caught up in the rapture, ecstasy, power, and release of such moments -- shower the 'prophet/leader/teacher' with adulation, reverence, gratitude, and love (i.e., provide narcissistic supply).

The seeker/follower interprets such moments as a validation of the idea that truth and spiritual transcendence are being channeled through the 'prophet/leader/teacher'. The 'prophet/teacher/guide' interprets such moments as a validation that he or she is who she or he believes himself/herself to be in the cosmic scheme of things and, therefore, that she or he has a right to the adulation and love that is being showered upon him/her.

Notwithstanding the foregoing considerations, one might still ask the question: What is the source of the charisma of a charismatic moment? Alternatively, what makes such moments charismatic?

If one defines charisma as the perceived embodiment of one's ultimate concerns, then seemingly, the charisma of a 'charismatic moment' would appear to be connected with the character of the experience that arises during that period of time. However, just because an experience is intense, powerful, inexplicable, mysterious, ineffable, emotionally moving, and ecstatic, does this necessarily make the experience a manifestation of the embodiment of one's ultimate concerns?

LSD, nitrous oxide, Ecstasy, alcohol, sensory deprivation, marijuana, giving birth, falling in love, and holotrophic breathing can all lead to experiences that bear many of the characteristics of so-called 'charismatic moments'. Many of the aforementioned, powerful, emotional qualities can be experienced when one looks up into the sky on a clear night sky and away from the city lights, or when one sees a range of mountains, or watches ocean waves come crashing into shore, or witnesses the power of nature in the form of a tornado, hurricane, lightening, volcanic eruption, or earthquake. The right musical, artistic, cinematic, literary settings or performances have the capacity to induce many of these same kinds of experiential qualities.

Charismatic moments can be manufactured or naturally occurring. These kinds of experience might, or might not, be about ultimate concerns, but, nonetheless, they have the capacity to move us in fundamental ways ... often in ways about which we might become uncertain or confused as to exactly why we might feel moved or affected in the way we are.

On several occasions, Oakes refers to the work of Charles Lindholm in relation to the phenomenon of charisma. According to Lindholm, the primary, but hidden, purpose of a charismatic group is not necessarily to help people to discover their essential spiritual identity or to realize ultimate spiritual concerns but, rather, to experience itself again and again as a certain kind of collective. Charismatic moments give expression to these kinds of experience.

In many ways, if the goal of a collection of people is to experience itself not just as a group but as a group that journeys through, or is opened up to, or is, to varying degrees, seeking to be immersed in intense, powerful, moving, primal, mysterious, emotional, joyous, ecstatic experiences, then the phenomenon of charisma -- whether manufactured, illusory, delusional, or real -- becomes the raison d'être underlying the structure, dynamics, and activities of the people in this sort of group. As such, certain kinds of experience become ends in themselves, rather than a possible means for struggling toward a spiritual understanding, knowledge, and insight concerning truths and realities that might transcend those experiences.

In such a context, 'charismatic prophets' are those individuals who serve as facilitators for arranging, manufacturing, and moving people in the direction of experiencing (or believing they are experiencing) charismatic moments. If this sort of facilitator is a narcissistic personality, then the idea of a charismatic moment becomes the bait that is used to lure people to help the 'prophet/leader/teacher' acquire what is necessary for his or her own charismatic moments ... namely, to feed off the souls of the people who wander into the vampire's lair. If the aforementioned facilitator is not a narcissistic personality, then one has to carefully study the dynamics and structure of the group with which such a facilitator is affiliated in order to determine whether the group has any constructive, spiritual purpose other than as a venue for generating certain kinds of experiences.

People who troll the waters of life seeking charismatic moments need to understand that there are other beings who are also trolling the waters of life, and these latter beings are trolling such waters in search of people who are trolling the waters seeking charismatic moments. If one is only seeking certain kinds of experiences -- described as charismatic, trans-personal, mystical, or altered states of consciousness -- and if one is not interested in gaining knowledge, understanding, and insight in order to become a better person with respect to developing and bringing into harmonious balance such character qualities as: patience, kindness, compassion, honesty, tolerance, love, forgiveness, fairness, generosity, integrity, nobility, peacefulness, altruism, modesty, and moral courage, then one is a very good candidate for winding up on a milk carton as a soul who has become lost or missing somewhere along the way.

Charismatic moments naturally lend themselves to becoming part of an intermittent, variable-interval reinforcement learning schedule in which the learned behaviors connected to seeking additional exposures to such moments can be very hard to extinguish once this sort of seeking behavior is set in motion. Once a person has had the experience of some sort of charismatic moment, this moment can be the point out of which emotional and psychological addiction arises.

In a sense, a narcissistic personality who is playing the role of a 'charismatic prophet' is pushing the charismatic moment like someone would push cocaine, heroin, or Ecstasy. The narcissistic personality is someone who, himself or herself, is addicted to a different drug -- namely, the narcissistic supply of adulation and surrender coming from others -- and the narcissistic personality uses this addiction to justify her or his efforts to make charismatic junkies of other human beings in order to preserve his or her own access to a constant source of narcissistic supply.

Irrespective of what one might believe about the existence of God or transcendent, spiritual truths, or the realization of essential identity and potential, a spiritual narcissist knows there are millions of people who do believe in such things ... each in his or her own way. This is the belief, this is the holy longing, to which a narcissistic, charismatic 'prophet/leader/guide' seeks to appeal and, subsequently, exploit or manipulate in the service of his or her pathology.

There is one other entry point to the issue of charisma that Oakes explores in an attempt to provide understanding with respect to the phenomenon of charisma. This additional avenue involves the work of Max Weber.

Although Oakes introduces his readers to the ideas of Weber fairly early in his book on Prophetic Charisma, I have left these ideas for the last part of the present essay. I have done this for a number of reasons but, perhaps, the primary one being that what Weber has to say dovetails with the way in which I wish to finish the discussion.

Oakes notes that Weber is the individual who is responsible for many of our modern ideas about the phenomenon of charisma. Weber describes charisma as a particular dimension of the personality of certain, special people that engenders in others a sense of feeling that the latter are in the presence of someone who is extraordinary, or someone who possesses supernatural capabilities, or someone who has some sort of close proximity and elevated status in relation to Divinity.

Weber indicates that charisma might be felt and manifested in non-religious contexts, but, nonetheless, he maintains that charisma is largely a religious or spiritual phenomenon. Furthermore, even though Weber was an advocate for seeking and providing social (rather than, say, psychological) explanations concerning the causes of a variety of individual and cultural dynamics, he also was of the opinion that ideas were capable of altering society and individuals in ways that could not be reduced down to purely social factors ... this was especially the case in conjunction with religious ideas.

According to Weber, the phenomenon of charisma gives expression to a continuum of possibilities. These range from: something that Weber referred to as 'pure charisma', to: relatively mechanical and derivative elements of charisma.

Weber considered instances of 'pure charisma' to be very rare and might only have been present during the very early, originating/creative stages in the formation of a group or movement when people first began to gather around a charismatic leader/personality. For Weber, the more routine manifestations of charisma usually arose after the founding force had passed away and/or when the original charisma had become diluted as that force is dispersed among secondary leaders and communities rather than being focused in one individual or the original group of followers.

320

On the one hand, Weber seems to believe that charisma was an expression of a fundamental, elemental, primitive life force. Yet, at the same time, Weber also appears to indicate that the source of charisma's capacity to influence resides as much in the power that followers cede to a leader as it does in the qualities of charisma that might be independent of such followers.

While it might be possible for a group of people to create the illusion of charisma being present in a given person when such is not the case (e.g., the manufactured charisma of celebrity status), nevertheless, presumably, there is a certain 'something' present in a charismatic individual that has the capacity to attract people and induce the latter to become inclined to place trust in that individual or to surrender, to varying degrees, to that individual. So, without wishing to dismiss the idea of manufactured charisma, Weber would seem to have something more in mind when he talks about 'pure charisma' -- 'something' that exists prior to, and independently of, group dynamics.

Somewhere between pure charisma and routine charisma lay several possibilities that Weber refers to, respectively, as 'magical' and 'prophetic' charisma. Magical charisma is said to be characteristic of shamans who use charisma to, on the one hand, introduce people to the realm of ecstasy, while, on the other hand, helping to maintain the basic structure of simple or primitive groups, communities, or society. As such, magical charisma is largely a conservative, stabilizing force.

Prophetic charisma is described by Weber as characteristic of more complex communities or societies. Such charisma supposedly is given expression through individuals who announce the sort of mission (often religious, but it could be political in nature) which is intended to lead to social change, if not revolution. Through a charismatic force of personality, and/or through the performance of miracles and wondrous deeds, and/or through a capacity to induce intense, passionate, and ecstatic experiences in others, a person who possesses prophetic charisma is capable of affecting other human beings in ways that run very deep emotionally, psychologically, physically, spiritually, and socially.

According to Weber, some charismatic personalities use charisma to assist others to become explorers of ecstatic mysteries. Some charismatic personalities, referred to as 'ethical prophets', use charisma as an ethical instrument intended to lead people in the direction of developing a life devoid of aggression, hatred, anger, fear, and violence by inducing states of euphoria, enlightenment, as well as what would now be termed 'born again' conversion experiences. Still other charismatic personalities seek to arouse, shape, and channel the passions of people to serve, whether for good or evil, various political, financial, and social ends.

Weber believes that the experience of intense, euphoric, passionate, ecstatic states comes about when charisma is used to put an individual in touch with his or her own inner psychological/emotional primeval, instinctual depths that enables an individual to break away from, or become released from, the inhibiting forces of convention and repression that normally hold people in place within a given society. As such, Weber maintains that charisma is a life force that is inherently antagonistic to the forces of inhibition, constraint, convention, and conservation that normally modulate the dynamics of social interaction. For Weber, the natural inclination of charisma is to seek to overthrow, transform, or cast off all external values of conventional society as charisma initiates individuals into that which is located beyond the horizons of traditional social structure ... something so 'other' that it is viewed as belonging to a Divine realm that transcends normal society and conventions.

Weber considered charisma to be: too irrational, unpredictable, unwieldy, and, therefore, dangerous to be tamed and controlled in any responsible fashion. Although he believed that charisma could serve as the creative spark that ignited the fires of social progress, he also was of the opinion that limiting the influence of charisma -

- at least in any 'pure' sense -- to the early period of originating or creating would be the prudent thing to do.

In the Islamic spiritual tradition, the Qur'an speaks about 'alastu bi rabikum' -- the time when, prior to being brought into this plane of existence, God gathered the spirits together and asked them: "Am I not your Lord?" Many other spiritual traditions allude to, and speak about, such a condition as well. Anything which resonates with that experience is believed to have a quality of jazb about it – that is, a euphoric, ecstatic condition as one is drawn back toward that moment, or as one is drawn toward a state that resonates, in some way, with that original, primal time of an aware, felt, intimate, loving, direct connection with the Divine presence.

From a mystical or spiritual perspective, authentic Prophets do not call us back to some biological state of the womb in which one, allegedly, felt one with the universe. Authentic Prophets do not call us back to some mythical state in which all boundaries between the mother and the self were dissolved so that the mother and the individual were felt to be as one, nor do authentic Prophets call us back to a condition of primary narcissism when, supposedly, we feel ourselves to be omnipotent, sacred, godlike creatures around which the universe rotates and in whose service the universe has come into existence, nor do authentic Prophets call us back to some instinctual,

primeval, emotional depths that is seeking to
release from the conventions and values of society.   324

Instead, authentic Prophets call us to seek the
truth concerning the purpose, meaning,
possibilities, dangers, and nature of existence.
Authentic Prophets call us to inquire into our
essential identities and potentials. Authentic
Prophets call us to honor the rights of all aspects of
creation, as well as to learn how to engage life
through justice, integrity, gratitude, love, sincerity,
courage, compassion, sacrifice, kindness, honesty,
patience, and humility. Authentic Prophets call us
to discover the true nature of our relationship with
all of Being and to go in search of the essential
meaning of worship.

From a mystical or spiritual point of view,
authentic Prophets are the individuals chosen by
Divinity who are provided with a charismatic
authoritativeness (said by traditions to consist of
forty-seven different parts, one of which concerns
the ability to provide correct interpretation of
dreams) as a Divine gift to enable such individuals
to carry out their mission, as best their individual
capacity and God permit, to call people back on a
journey of return to their spiritual origins, nature,
identity, purpose, potential, and destiny. In such
individuals, charisma is the felt manifestation of the
presence of this Divine gift.

If one accepts the principle that there is no
reality but Divinity, then the passion play of Divine
Names and Attributes forms the woof, warp, and

fabric through which the tapestry of creation and every modality of manifestation is woven. Everything to which we are attracted bears, to one degree or another, the imprint of the underlying Reality.

As such, there are many kinds of charisma. There is a form of charisma associated with every manner in which Divinity discloses something of the Divine Presence. Natural wonders the mysterious, incredible athletic performances, great musical or artistic talent, literary masterpieces, extraordinary heroic deeds, works of great intelligence or profound inventiveness and creativity … all of these attract according to the degree that they give manifestation to the charisma inherent in the Divine Presence that is peeking through the veils of Creation.

Power carries an aura of charisma because it is God's will that enables someone to ascend to the throne of power. Even Satanic power and capabilities might have a quality of charisma to them because such powers and capabilities are exercised only by God's leave and that serve -- in a way that God understands but Satanic forces do not -- Divine purposes.

The natural inclination inherent in the pure charisma that is given expression through the lives of authentic Prophets is constructive, not destructive. It is benevolent, not malevolent … it is peaceful, not aggressive and hostile … it is committed to the distribution of fairness, justice, and the honoring of the rights of all facets of Creation, rather than given to the generation of upheaval, discord, and rebellion ... it is oriented toward the acquisition of essential knowledge, wisdom and understanding through which the constructive potential of life, both individually and collectively, can be released and set free, rather than being oriented toward primitive forms of physical and emotional release associated with the individual desires, whims, and wishes of the carnal soul.

If God wishes, authentic Prophetic charisma offers spiritual nourishment to both individuals and communities. God willing, people become strengthened and constructively energized through the presence of authentic Prophetic charisma.

The desire to be in the presence of authentic Prophetic charisma is part of the holy longing that seeks to feel re-connected, in an intimate way, with the Divine. From the standpoint of traditional spirituality, authentic Prophetic charisma is the catalyst provided by Divinity that is intended to help facilitate such a connection and return.

It is unfortunate that Oakes has used the term 'prophetic charisma' to refer primarily to pathological attempts to counterfeit authentic expressions of 'prophetic charisma'. This has happened, I believe, because the sample that Oakes used to develop his notion of a prophet was problematic and skewed in certain, problematic directions.

The 'package' of qualities that is manifested through narcissistic personalities attempting to convince others (and themselves) that they possess the charisma of an authentic Prophet is but a counterfeit of the qualities that are in evidence in an authentic Prophet. This package is an illusory/delusional framework that is intended to create an impression that qualities like: confidence, purpose, strength, courage, fearlessness, meaning, identity, love, social insight, creativity, powers of communication, persuasiveness, transformation, and transcendent experiences of spiritual ecstasy are present in an authentic, sacred way when such is not the case.

Quite frequently, when people encounter spiritual abuse, this experience tends to destroy a person's faith and capacity to trust. Once one has felt betrayed in an essential way -- which is at the heart of all forms of spiritual abuse -- regaining a sincere desire to continue on one's quest to realize one's holy longing is very difficult to do.

A mistake that many people make who write about spiritual abuse is to approach the issue from an excessively rational, philosophical, and psychological perspective ... one which seems to tend to preclude the possibility that the phenomenon of Prophetic charisma -- as an expression of the Presence of Divinity in our midst and which is inviting us to a journey of return to our spiritual potential and essential identities -- is not a myth, fantasy, delusion, or mere belief.

Although I believe that Oakes' work on 'Prophetic Charisma' contains much that is interesting, insightful, and useful, I also feel that, ultimately, his study fails to place the phenomenon of charisma in a proper spiritual perspective. One of the reasons why narcissistic personalities can fool people -- and some narcissists are much better at this than are others -- is because individuals in the throes of narcissistic personality disorder are able to turn people's natural vulnerabilities concerning issues of holy longing against the latter.

In other words, even when someone seeks the sacred out of a sincere desire for the truth and not out of the 'extraordinary needs' of, say, unresolved, developmental issues involving the alleged infantile stage of primary narcissism, nonetheless, such an individual doesn't really know precisely for what he or she is longing. There are many kinds of experiences and circumstances that can resonate with the condition of -- 'alastu bi rabikum (Am I not your Lord)? -- in a misleading manner.

A narcissistic personality who is trying to pass herself or himself off as a charismatic prophet/leader/teacher knows that seekers don't know -- that is why the latter group of people are seeking answers from others about how to satisfy their sense of holy longing ... because they don't know how to do this on their own. Even in the case of sincere people, what the latter sort of individuals don't know constitutes a source of vulnerability through which such sincerity can be misinformed, led astray, corrupted, or entangled in a variety of ways.

Narcissistic personalities are often masters at re-framing experience to make it appear to be other than what it is. Satan is the prototypic role model for such a narcissistic personality disorder.

At one point, Oakes mentions that in 'The Heart of Darkness' Joseph Conrad, through the character Marlow, suggests that a "fool is always safe". In other words, an individual who doesn't care about the holy longing within, who is not sincere about matters of essential importance to existence, will rarely be fooled by those who -- through manufactured or natural charisma of one kind or another -- seek to use the attractiveness of such charisma to mislead people into supposing that something essentially substantial is being offered when such is not the case. Fools are always safe from being misled in this manner because they have no interest in, and feel no attraction for, things that actually matter.

Intelligent, sincere, decent people are vulnerable to the presence of counterfeit spiritual charisma. Mistakes of judgment concerning whether, or not, some individual is capable of helping one fulfill one's holy longing are relatively easy to make, and, unfortunately, once made, not all of these mistakes admit to easy solutions.

Short of God's Grace, there is no fool-proof way to identify or avoid narcissistic personalities who seek to prey on holy longing. However, one point that might well be worth reflecting on in this respect is the following -- any use of charisma that invites one to abandon basic principles of decency, kindness, honesty, integrity, compassion, generosity, fairness, modesty, humility, patience, tolerance, forgiveness, peacefulness, and love toward one's family or other human beings irrespective of the beliefs of the latter, should be considered to be a tell-tale sign that spiritual abuse is being perpetrated. This is so no matter how euphoric and ecstatic various 'charismatic moments' might be that are associated with such a use of charisma.

There is a fundamental problem inherent in any use of charisma that does not assist one to become a better human being, with a more fully developed and realized moral character that is encouraged to be actively practiced and not just thought about as an abstract ideal. However, sometimes -- depending on the forces at play in a given set of circumstances and depending on the skills of the narcissistic perpetrator who is busy weaving a tapestry of illusions, delusions, and manipulative deceit -- discovering that such a problem exists can be a long difficult process, and, furthermore, disengaging from such circumstances once this problem has been discovered is not necessarily an easy, painless, straightforward thing to accomplish. Indeed, sometimes, long after one has left a narcissistic personality who has been posing as a charismatic prophet, remnants of the toxicity continue to flow through one's system ...

not because one wishes this to be the case but because this is often part and parcel of the destructive, insidious nature of the ramifications ensuing from spiritual abuse.

331